# Poor
# No
# More

# Poor No More

## Rethinking Dependency and the War on Poverty

## Peter Cove

**Transaction Publishers**
New Brunswick (U.S.A.) and London (U.K.)

Library of Congress Catalog Number: 2016036361
ISBN: 978-1-4128-6434-3 (hardcover); 978-1-4128-6445-9 (paperback)
eBook: 978-1-4128-6449-7
Printed in the United States of America

Library of Congress Cataloging-in-Publication Data

Names: Cove, Peter, author.
Title: Poor no more : rethinking dependency and the war on poverty / Peter Cove.
Description: New Brunswick, NJ : Transaction Publishers, [2017]
Identifiers: LCCN 2016036361| ISBN 9781412864343 (hardcover : alk. paper) | ISBN 9781412864459 (pbk. : alk. paper)
Subjects: LCSH: Poverty–Government policy–United States. | Economic assistance, Domestic–United States. | Public welfare–United States. | Poor–United States.
Classification: LCC HC110.P63 C69 2017 | DDC 362.5/5610973–dc23 LC record available at https://lccn.loc.gov/2016036361

To my wife, Lee, partner and muse, the force making America Works the most successful company of its kind in the United States.

# Contents

# Foreword: 250 Broadway, New York City, Spring 2009

I sit in the studio provided for my three-week residency by the Rockefeller Foundation overlooking the spectacular Lake Como. The irony of writing about poverty while in residence in this glorious and supportive environment is not lost on me. As I think about the solution I have come up with to solve poverty in America, I recall the last sentence of the poem "Skipper Ireson's Ride" that I was required to learn in high school in Marblehead, MA, in 1957. I expect that like Ireson, I will be "tarred and feathered and carried in a cart by the women of Marblehead." Not just Marblehead, I suppose.

I grew up with the smell of hot lead burning my nostrils as it miraculously left my father, Sam, unscathed as he picked up the metal type. Years of picking up the red hot lines of type had rendered him immune to the blazing heat. He and my Uncle Chap ran the linotype machine, a monstrous typewriter, seven feet tall sporting all the gears and gizmos befitting the mechanical creations of the nineteenth-century Industrial Revolution. Sam sat in front of this Rube Goldberg machine and would type in lines that would find their way onto my grandfather's table where he would compose pages from the type and wooden blocks with copper pictures that would be placed on a large printer (he was a compositor, the highest level of printmaking in its day). These lines of type—thus the line-o-type machine—were six or seven inch slugs of metal drawn mechanically from a pot of melted lead that then formed sentences in a remarkable process similar to using a mold to form impressions. I would sit next to him, this product of the Depression, sweating in a tee shirt and jeans, and marvel at his energy and enthusiasm for his work. Only now, realizing that he had a master's degree, does his blue collar profession at the time seem somewhat out of place. But his stories of the Depression explain it all. He was deathly afraid of joblessness and the poverty in which he grew up. He would tell of being so hungry as a paperboy that on winter mornings he would scrape the frozen cream off bottles of milk on the stoops that had bulged out of their bottles.

What I saw in my father, uncle, and grandfather, printers all, was a dedication to work, though I did not know that then. And perhaps I saw people who had witnessed joblessness and poverty and were damned if they would let that happen again. Looking back, my father was willing to take any job after the war to support his family, regardless of his higher educational achievements. My grandfather, in a different era, might well have been a professional—of what I am unsure, although he taught me magic, how to fish, and how to command an audience. He schooled me in how to tell a joke. He was the smartest man in the room, any room. He was my idol. I have a picture of him, pipe in mouth, looking up from his large compositor's table, slyly grinning at the camera with an almost "you could never do what I am doing here" expression. He worked hard to achieve his station in his brother's printing plant on Atlantic Avenue in Boston and he plied the trade with brimming enthusiasm—almost the same as that for his pinochle games. With only a sixth grade education but aware of his intelligence, he never envied those who might have what he was unable to obtain.

The importance of work seeped into my blood without my being aware of it—just as a medicine, added to an intravenous without your knowing, alters the body's chemistry.

My wife, Dr. Lee Bowes, and I have spent decades establishing programs to reduce poverty, putting them to the test, and discarding those that did not work. In the 1970s and 1980s we ran education and training programs that were intended to reduce dependence on welfare. At the time, the accepted view was that the best method for moving mothers on welfare[1] into jobs was by investing in human capital—that is, by providing these individuals with education, training, and work experience before anything else. Work experience did not work because it was premised on the idea that people were not ready for work in the real world. So the "experience" was separate from jobs at companies and generally a poor substitute for the real world. After years of trying, we finally had to face the truth: these programs simply did not work. We were dramatically more successful in reducing dependence when we focused on placing a candidate in a job first, and then investing in human capital to move that person up in wages and position. We tested both schemes, and the differences were stark: where human capital failed, work-first succeeded.

Yet our findings were anathema to policy-makers of the day. One of the preeminent figures in welfare policy, New York Senator Daniel Patrick Moynihan, was a firm believer that education and training should come first. In 1989, I testified at a Senate hearing he chaired during which I strongly urged adopting a work-first policy, rather than one that emphasized education and training—that is, what policy-makers refer to as the human capital approach. He was tepid in his public response, but after the hearing we adjourned to his office only to be berated for not accepting the human capital first argument that he preferred. I had similar encounters after that with Paul Offner, his chief of staff. Only after many years did Offner confront me in the senator's office and say, "Well, Cove, you were right." In 2004, the very research organization that Senator Moynihan and others had relied upon for welfare policy, Manpower Demonstration Research Corporation (MDRC), finally admitted that the human capital approach was not a good first strike in moving people off the welfare rolls. Work-first, on the other hand, worked.[2]

We went on to work with the Clinton White House and Newt Gingrich, then the Speaker of the House, to adopt work-first as a guiding tenet of the Personal Responsibility and Work Opportunity Act of 1996. That legislation substantially helped the country to reduce the welfare rolls by over 60 percent in the following twelve years—perhaps the most successful public policy achievement in the nation's history.[3]

Work-first was successful in 1996—and has remained so over the past two decades—but there is still much to be done. Poverty remains rife in America, and the White House, along with many state houses, persists in its old fashioned ideas about how to connect poor people to jobs.

What I am proposing in this book is a radical solution to poverty in America, grounded in my five decades of experience on the front lines. This will not be a cookbook of programs, with each recipe designed to tackle some specific cause of poverty. Instead it will offer a wholesale redesign of how we wage our war. Simply, I propose that we eliminate all welfare programs except those geared toward people who truly cannot work due to physical or mental problems.[4] Second, we scuttle *all* poverty programs, including everything from Head Start to Food Stamps. From 1964 until today we have spent over $19 trillion on such programs and have hardly moved the poverty rate down from 17 percent in 1965 to 14.5 percent in 2014.[5] We should wipe the slate clean, take all the money saved, and create jobs—first, in the private sector and then, as a last resort, in the public one. In so doing we will return our country to a work ethic and steer it away from dependency. We will solve poverty with work—a job for all who are able.

Not everyone will be receptive to the changes I am proposing. There will be those who will cling to old ideological and political biases. Unable to see the truth about their long-held ideas on fighting poverty and how they have failed, they will argue that the propositions set forth here will be harmful— even cruel. The alternatives may superficially appear more humane, but the truth is that they simply have not worked. Why? Because their "humaneness" underestimates the poor's capacity to go to work.

In medicine there is a term *iatrogenic*, which is used to describe an adverse condition that results from an action of the physician. The Hippocratic Oath cautions doctors to first do no harm. If a doctor found he was responsible for a patient's iatrogenic condition, he must abandon the harmful treatment. A patient's health is far more important than medical dogma.

In social policy, no such modus operandi exists. As Lee and I have seen firsthand, even evidence-based research is generally ineffective in altering public policy regardless of the facts. Ideology trumps efficacy. And the poor continue to suffer.

On the move now are social policies based on progressivism. As practiced by our current president and Bill de Blasio, elected in 2014 as mayor of the City of New York, we are returning to the failed programs and approaches of the past. Mayor de Blasio proposes what may seem to be a "kinder, gentler welfare system" (along with a kinder, gentler police department). While some isolated changes might have potential, the truth is that if taken to an extreme, we could find ourselves returning to the old, free-spending days of the 1960s, when New York Welfare Commissioner Mitchell

Ginsberg was dubbed "Come and get it Ginsberg." Such trends are playing out on both the national and local levels, as President Obama and the mayor are rejecting the welfare bill of 1996's mandate for reciprocal responsibility. Even in Wisconsin, ground zero for welfare reform under Governor Tommy Thompson in the 1990s, welfare recipients are no longer sanctioned for lack of participation in work. Specifically, they have eliminated the requirement that people on Food Stamps work if there is a job and they are able-bodied. These and other U-turns in welfare policy portend a rise in dependence and in poverty.

Nevertheless, I am an optimist. Perhaps, in light of the mounting failures of the past decades, our country might finally be ready to take a long, hard look at welfare policy and human nature. Perhaps our leaders are ready to admit that the repetition of the same self-defeating action is a definition of lunacy. And perhaps, we will look at the problem straight on and make the difficult choices necessary to reverse this appalling situation.

Why would anyone support policies that have proven, time and again, not only ineffective, but actually harmful? Why have liberals, avowed defenders of the downtrodden, continued to advocate for failed programs? Because making real change threatens the foundations of their own electoral support. Because defending the vulnerable is ultimately less important than kowtowing to labor unions, social workers, community groups, and the welfare-industrial complex. They have thrown the poor under the special interest bus.

Unfortunately, conservatives have been little better. For decades they have ceded poverty policy to the liberals. Content to criticize welfare queens, growing dependency, and increased government without providing new solutions of their own, they have added little to the debate. Both sides have chosen to score political points rather than make hard choices.

The solution is a simple one. Work must replace dependency. Getting to that answer took me decades of trial and error—and a certain openness to challenging ideology. I pray that after years of crisis and failure, changing the course of public policy will not take decades more.

## Notes

1. I say "mothers on welfare" because the Aid to Families with Dependent Children (AFDC) program, which existed from 1935 to 1996, was originally designed to provide relief to single mothers—as such, these were the primary recipients of welfare at the time.

2. Judith M. Gueron and Howard Rolston, *Fighting For Reliable Evidence* (New York: Russell Sage Foundation, 2013), 296.

3. Bill Clinton, "How We Ended Welfare, Together," http://www.nytimes.com/2006/08/22/opinion/22clinton.html?_r=0.

4. I am excepting the Earned Income Tax Credit (EITC), the Child Tax Credit (CTC), and other refundable tax credits, which do much to encourage work.

5. Michael Tanner and Charles Hughes, "The War on Poverty Turns 50," *Policy Analysis*, no. 761 (Washington, DC: Cato Institute, October 20, 2014), 3. This figure is in constant 2014 dollars.

# Acknowledgments

Although fifty years of experience were necessary for me to organize this book's analysis and conclusions, there are so many people who have influenced my thinking and assisted me in its completion.

Dr. Lee Bowes, my wife and the CEO of America Works, whose staggering intelligence and superb judgment have led our company, and those we serve, to success. Her significant ideas and constant review of the drafts made this a much better book.

Fred Siegel, my dear friend and a vital mentor for both me and America Works, is a man for whom I have only the deepest affection, respect, and gratitude. I cannot count the times during this book's gestation I have called on this great historian and social commentator for advice and fact checking. His wife, Jan Rosenberg, has been tireless in her support of America Works and its mission and a superb critic and advisor on the manuscript.

Before anyone else, Professor Larry Mead recognized welfare's underbelly and became for many of us a beacon of sanity for social policy. Larry's work with me on this book has strengthened it enormously. He called me out when one fact or another just did not seem to have support and added substantively to historical and policy discussions.

Thanks to the Manhattan Institute (MI), for first publishing the article in *City Journal* that became the basis of this book. Larry Mone, president, and Brian Anderson, editor of

*City Journal*, were enthusiastic supporters of my ideas and this project. Bernadette Seton, MI's book representative for her guidance. It has been a privilege for Lee and me to be able to work with Larry on a number of joint projects between The Manhattan Institute and America Works.

In addition, there are other Manhattan Institute scholars and writers who have influenced my thinking as I have grown to reject much of that which we thought would solve poverty and propose a new way. These include my friend Kay Hymowitz, whose important social commentary on family and marriage has had a strong impact on my thinking; Sol Stern, who helped craft my *City Journal* article and continues to maintain his position as one of America's great critics on educational policy; John McWhorter, who has written so intelligently on race in America; Howard Hussock, for his incisive commentaries on housing; and Heather McDonald, one of the most passionate and combative writers on welfare, police, and race in America today. It was after reading Howard's piece alongside Nathan Glazer's "The Limits of Social Policy" that Lee and I first went to have lunch with Professor Glazer, whose insights are reflected in my thinking even though I am uncertain he would agree with all my conclusions. Theodore Dalrymple's writings in *City Journal* and elsewhere have likewise been crucial as I crafted my perspective on policy issues. Charles Murray's initial salvo at the War on Poverty set the standard for the critical analysis of its failures. Without the support of The Manhattan Institute his insights in Losing Ground might never have seen the light of day.

Herb London, now director of the London Center, has been of tremendous assistance to me personally and to America Works generally over the years. His intellect is awesome and as broad as anyone I know. This manuscript would likely never have seen the light of day had it not been for his help in interesting Transaction Publishers to introduce this book.

Arthur Brooks, President of the American Enterprise Institute (AEI), has afforded me many ideas in his writings, of which perhaps the most important is an answer to the question of why conservatives tend to lose arguments to liberals. (Spoiler alert: it is because they argue facts, while liberals play to emotion.)

David Stove's *What's Wrong with Benevolence* so altered my thinking about how to handle poverty that his influence cannot be overestimated. Much of this book relies upon his insights.

James Q. Wilson's vision, including his Broken Windows theory, contributed massively to my understandings of behavior and society. His passing leaves an enormous void in social intelligent and transformative commentary.

Herb Sturtz as head of The Vera Institute influenced how I created America Works. His devotion to honest research to determine if his programs worked became a mantra for me.

Two politicians who truly got what was wrong with welfare policy and changed it were Bill Clinton and Rudy Guiliani. President Clinton once remarked to Lee and me, "There should be an America Works in every city in the US." And he adopted the work-first model we advised the White House on for the welfare reform of 1996. It is my hope this will come to pass. Mayor Giuliani has stated that his changes to welfare policy in New York City might never have happened if it were not for his visit to our company and our counsel. His efforts reduced New York's welfare population by well over 50 percent.

I have quoted Joe Klein in this book and it is not just because he is a friend. He is perhaps our preeminent reporter and journalist—the commentator of our age. He also knows music like no one else (read his outstanding biography of Woody Guthrie).

David Osborn in his book *Reinventing Government* was the first to point out that America Works was a reinventing government company, playing a part in a movement we only later came to fully recognize. Elaine Kamark, now at Brookings, played a critical role on Vice President Al Gore's staff by helping to successfully introduce these ideas about reinventing government into the federal bureaucracy.

There are many people who have helped with this book's creation. Russell Sykes and Bob Scardamalia contributed analysis essential to supporting this book's assertion that we could accomplish my objectives to eliminate poverty. Rus was also instrumental in helping me find some accommodation between a work-first policy and intelligent education and training. Anthony Bozza, my researcher, worked with diligence and intelligence to gather data and analysis, particularly concerning the rise of dependency and its causes.

The Rockefeller Foundation awarded me a stay at their Residence in Bellagio, Italy, during which I drafted the article for *City Journal* upon which the arguments in this book were created.

Henry Saltzman and Jerry Wishnow, both old friends, have offered advice and commentary throughout the writing of the book.

Two former Commissioners of The Human Resources Administration for New York City offered me invaluable guidance. Robert Doar provided me the insight that we have in large part replaced poverty with dependency. And Jason Turner, among many other things, demonstrated why my proposals would work. His thinking is incorporated in my last chapter. I could ask for no better assurance.

The late Governor Mario Cuomo first helped us establish our company in New York City and his son, Andrew, the current governor, as well has supported our efforts. Congressman Paul Ryan, former Congressman Steve Southerland, and Speaker Gingrich each in their special way have supported our efforts at getting people to work.

It was the Progressive Policy Institute, part of The Democratic Leadership Committee, through Will Marshall and Bruce Reed that convinced President Clinton to adopt the work-first approach in the welfare bill of 1996 replacing the failed education and training strategies that had failed.

Tim DeWerff conducted the first and difficult edits on the book. His courage to challenge me and his meticulous scrutiny of this book's contents contributed enormously to its completion.

Early stages of the book were helped by the suggestions of my friend, the great historian, Thomas Fleming who taught this first time book writer how to organize and think about narrative.

Brandon Proia, who edited my first and second and third drafts. He did a remarkable job of saving my thoughts from the trash heap of history by making them readable and hopefully compelling. This book would have been so much less without his singular editorial assistance.

This book would likely have not seen the light of day without the help of Herb London.

Family support has been crucial. We are fortunate that our daughter Antonia has joined the management of America Works and Dirrane has taken on the executive director's position of the Work First Foundation, a laboratory for generating new and innovative employment programs. Also, my daughter Amanda's commitment to social work continues our concern for people in need. My sons Louis and David, while taking different paths, continue to give me pride in their accomplishments.

Lastly to the talented and devoted staff of America Works who with the utmost passion make Lee's and my mission succeed. I could name names, but the enormous list would cause sleepiness. Just one—Phil Jones, the heart of our company, there almost from the beginning, loved by all and my soul brother. He exemplifies the best of America Works.

# Introduction

Nearly half a century ago, I dropped out of graduate school and enlisted as a foot soldier in America's War on Poverty. Today, I'm still on the front lines, working to move people out of dependency and into employment. But with an important difference: I have become fed up with the piecemeal and impotent policies that I once supported, and I'm now trying to change the strategy of our bogged-down army.

Life sneaks up on you. One day you are tight, taut, and tousled with hair that glows and grows. Then, what once was taken for granted recedes, giving way to the sculpting of time. The person you are now has crept up, unpredictable but inevitable. The physical change slaps you in the face—one day you look in the mirror and find you are no longer fighting pimples but gravity. However, the changes inside your head, the emotions, and intellectual aging blossom more slowly, imperceptibly until suddenly they become very consequential indeed. Only when I began to recognize that the social policy that was powering my work had drifted from a left perspective to a more conservative one did I come to the epiphany that I had changed.

Looking in the rearview mirror at my life, there are at least three signal events that have permanently changed my thinking about how to fight poverty. Luckily, at these moments I was open to reflection. I challenged my own ideology and firmly held beliefs. This is a summation of how and why my thinking about poverty changed.

1

What first opened my eyes was a job I took in the mid-1970s at the Vera Institute of Justice in New York, led by the brilliant policy innovator Herbert Sturtz. While at Vera, Sturtz had created small experimental programs aimed at reducing crime. He studied them scientifically, sometimes with control and experimental groups and, if they proved successful, asked governments or foundations to take them on and expand them. One of these experimental programs, the Wildcat Services Corporation, was running employment programs for the most hard-to-place welfare recipients across the five boroughs. My role would be to serve as head of two of Wildcat's five borough offices.

The experience was revelatory. At Wildcat, we found that the best way to get clients off welfare was to find them paid work immediately, rather than enrolling them in training and education programs. I saw with my own eyes the value of work—any kind of paid work—in reducing welfare dependency and attacking poverty. I learned that if we helped welfare clients get jobs, even entry-level jobs, they would then attend to their other needs. Here is a perfect example. When some mothers on welfare came to us, they often explained that they could not work because they had no day care. We would still send them on a job interview, and when the company wanted to hire them, miraculously, they found a grandmother or daycare center. Childcare wasn't ultimately the problem—it was their insecurity about being worth anything in the private marketplace. Once they were offered a job, all the barriers to work fell away. By contrast, if the government continued giving them money and other benefits, they were likely to remain dependent.

The reasons should have been obvious. Work maximizes a person's capacity to achieve economic self-reliance. Work socializes people and instills a sense of personal responsibility in them. Work demonstrates that behavior has consequences.

And it allows people to feel the pride and self-respect that come with supporting their spouses and children.

Another of Vera's signature achievements was its practice of conducting research on its own initiatives, something practically unheard of at the time (and rare even today). The operators of antipoverty programs typically shy away from serious empirical research. Such programs were primarily run by people with an ideological belief in the redemptive power of their own programs, and measuring their success, or lack thereof, threatened to undermine that belief.[1] Some might argue that exposing even a small flaw would be used by opponents to cut their funding, but I would disagree. I have never found that admitting program inadequacies based on research and adjusting the strategies accordingly was self-destructive—in fact, it is crucial to improving policy and achieving success. This is why we have always run research on our own programs and adjusted as needed with no fallout in support. It is a self-regulating quality control mechanism.

The second "aha" moment came in 1972 when I had a conversation with Mitchell ("Mike") Sviridoff, then a high-ranking official at the Ford Foundation. He had funded Vera and the start-up of Wildcat and had been enormously influential in pioneering programs in the 1950s that would become the models for many of those in the national War on Poverty.

As we discussed our job placement program, I said, "Mike, what we are showing is that there should be jobs for all." His response was vehement: "Don't you ever say that publicly. NEVER!" I was shocked, confused, and mystified. It was only recently, while testing the proposals outlined in this book, did I come to understand what might have motivated Mike to respond so passionately to what seemed to me a perfectly reasonable statement of fact. JOBS FOR ALL was a catch-phrase used by proponents of socialism, and he did not want to be seen as aligned with that kind of thinking.

I was having a talk with Steve Greenhouse, a superbly talented journalist then working for the *New York Times*. I wanted to see if my proposals would be rejected by someone more liberal than myself—which Steve is. After I briefly outlined my ideas, Steve said, to my shock, "Well, Peter, you are just proposing socialism, a job for all." At that moment the meaning of Mike's furious reaction became clear. Mike was born, bred, and worked as a union organizer steeped in the drift of far left thinking. To create socialism in America was, in fact, exactly what he was driving at. By shutting me down, he was telling me not to expose the leftist ideology of the programs. It took me forty years to understand this. And, as you will see, this ideology affected the design of the poverty programs that were destined to fail. It was to attack poverty from an altogether different perspective that I set up a for-profit company based on work-first and paid for results. These were conservative approaches to the liberal notion of helping people better themselves.

The third and final moment came more recently. In the mid-1990s, I was being interviewed on NBC. The interviewer asked a question that went something like this: "Mr. Cove, in the 60s you were antiwar, against segregation, and an active supporter of the War on Poverty. You believed business was inherently corrupt. Would the Peter Cove of the 60s like the Peter Cove of today?" Momentarily stunned by the question I answered no. The enormity of how far I had traveled came crashing in to me at that moment.

I have spent more than fifty years working to help the poor. Though I began as a true believer in the War on Poverty, the more time I spent in the field, the more aware I became of just how miserably our efforts had failed. Today's poverty rate of 14.5 percent, by the official federal poverty measure, is little changed from the rate of 17.3 percent that prevailed in 1965 when I began—yet we had spent more than $20 trillion to alleviate it.[2]

In 1984, based on the work my wife, Lee Bowes, and I had done in Boston, I created a for-profit company, America Works, to put these theories into action. America Works offers employment services to state and local welfare agencies with the aim of placing welfare recipients in jobs quickly, with a minimal amount of time spent on training. My wife quickly became the CEO and has been responsible for its tremendous success. Thanks to her, America Works has placed hundreds of thousands of people into jobs throughout the United States.

Around the same time, the state of Wisconsin was implementing work-first approaches as part of their welfare reform.[3] But even there, conventional wisdom held that there was no place for a private, for-profit venture in the antipoverty field. Most activists believed that helping welfare recipients was God's work, that making a profit was inherently wrong, and that a private company would inevitably seek to increase profits by reducing services to the poor. Ohio was one of the few exceptions to this, hiring America Works to run an experimental welfare program. I got a boost, from Ohio Governor Richard Celeste, who let me secure a contract from his state's social-services department to open welfare-to-work programs in Cleveland and Dayton. With that contract in hand, I raised $1 million in start-up money, betting that a for-profit company could do the job better than government welfare agencies could, by bringing accountability to a field that desperately needed it. Operating out of corporate offices in Boston, MA, I found little enthusiasm for my approach among my peers. As Larry Mone, president of the Manhattan Institute says, "In Boston, they don't so much disagree with you, they disapprove of you." Their disapproval was palpable.

America Works staked its survival—and my reputation—on the proposition that welfare clients, properly motivated and helped with a limited amount of technical assistance alongside tons of support, could be successful at finding and holding jobs. Our typical contract stipulates that we don't get paid our full fee until we place a client in a job and the client completes a successful probationary period of four to six months. This arrangement motivates our trainers and employment specialists to perform well; they understand that if they are unsuccessful with job placements, we'll lose a sizable amount of money, our contract will be cancelled, and we'll be out of a job ourselves.

Our experience has confirmed that the main obstacles (besides the government itself) preventing welfare clients from finding and retaining jobs are a lack of professional connections (we kidded and called ourselves the old girls network) and large gaps in interpersonal skills. That in and of itself explains why extended education and training programs are unnecessary time-consuming diversions—clients with shaky self-confidence are best served by early success in getting a job, not by long periods of preparation. Our weeklong training sessions are narrowly focused on the attributes and skills needed to land an entry-level job. Our trainers work with clients on the basics, such as maintaining a businesslike personal appearance, speaking properly, preparing a résumé, and showing up on time. Clients quickly learn that success depends on self-discipline and their own motivation and effort.

Over the past three decades our approach has led to the placement of over a half million poor people in private-sector jobs, with an average starting wage of over $10 per hour plus benefits, at the time of this writing.[4] Before coming to us, those clients spent an average of five years on the welfare rolls. In our New York City program, more than half of these new workers were still employed after 180 days. We have placed workers with prestigious companies such as Time Warner, Cablevision, Aramark, J. C. Penney, and American Building Maintenance Industries. Most of these employers keep coming back, asking for more of our referrals.

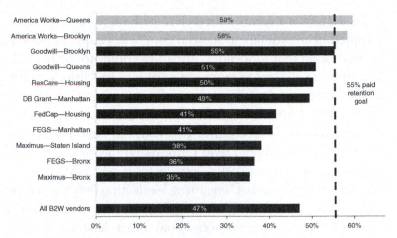

**Figure I.1**[5]. Retention rates for workers, 180 days after being placed in jobs by various programs in New York City. As is clear from the above, America Works is regularly among the most effective at placing individuals in jobs for the long term, exceeding the established goal of 55 percent retention. Graph produced by the NYC Human Resources Administration research office.

With our help, single parents, drug and alcohol abusers, the mentally handicapped, the homeless, military veterans with posttraumatic stress disorder, and others have succeeded admirably in a wide variety of jobs and have lifted themselves out of a lifetime of poverty.

One of the first political leaders who supported America Works was New York Governor and Democrat Mario Cuomo. He was passionate about the value of work. Whenever he was asked to speak to a group of welfare recipients, he would throw away his speech and speak from the heart about how his parents emigrated from Italy and found themselves on welfare. He would talk about the shop owners who gave the family employment and how it gave them dignity and respect. There was never a dry eye in the house, and the audience would rush to speak to him. It was he who crossed the political aisle to join the new Mayor Guiliani and come to the America Works offices for a doubling of the size of America Works.

Yet despite our admirable track record, we were never fully accepted by the welfare-industrial complex. People persisted in their belief that for-profit companies could not be trusted and that the classroom trumped working. In Ohio, county welfare offices and traditional social-services agencies flexed their political muscles and successfully lobbied the state to discontinue our contract after two years. In New York City, during the mayoralty of David Dinkins, city agencies rejected our bids for welfare-to-work contracts four consecutive times. We were even accused of "creaming"—selecting only the ablest clients, who would have landed jobs on their own anyway. However, two careful evaluations showed that American Works produces superior results even controlling for the features of the clients.[6] But people remained suspicious of our methods and continued to attack our for-profit business model.

Even the liberal media began to criticize me and America Works. Never mind that we were helping poor people get good jobs—I was committing an act of heresy by using a for-profit company and rejecting classroom training.

Nevertheless, we persevered.

We achieved a breakthrough with the election of Rudy Giuliani as New York's mayor in 1993. Lee and I had first met him after he lost the previous election to Dinkins. Giuliani was initially skeptical that it was possible to move long-term welfare clients so quickly into employment and that there were so many companies willing—even eager—to hire them. But then he made a visit to our offices and became convinced.

In his two terms as mayor, Giuliani reduced the welfare rolls by more than half a million people.[7] He did this, in large part, by emphasizing work-based programs. At a celebration for the twenty-fifth anniversary of America Works six years ago, Giuliani recalled a Gotham that had encouraged welfare dependency. He talked of families going into a second and third generation, in many cases, of people who hadn't worked, who didn't know the experience of work. He realized that the welfare programs run by the city, the state, and the federal government all actually incentivized welfare. Naturally, welfare rolls increased in response. As their programs grew, government staff got bigger offices, bigger titles, and more money. In essence, failure in the lives of the people became success for the welfare worker. Giuliani ended by observing that he probably never would have thought of his own work program if he had not gone to America Works.

Giuliani's success in reducing welfare caseloads soon reached Washington. In his campaign, President Clinton promised to "end welfare as we know it." His reform plan, he said, would transform welfare from a way of life into a "second chance" on the way to employment. The following year, he signed the Republican Personal Responsibility and Work Opportunity Reconciliation Act (the program called TANF), the biggest change in welfare programs since President Roosevelt's New Deal. Welfare activists and many Democrats were aghast at the mandatory work requirements in the legislation, as well as its threat that people who didn't actively move toward employment could be kicked off the rolls. Even Senator Daniel Patrick Moynihan, no bleeding-heart liberal, famously predicted that "children will be sleeping on the grates" of sidewalks.[8]

But such dire warnings were off the mark. Welfare reform embraced the work-first ideal—at least in part—and the results were nothing short of remarkable. Welfare rolls plummeted from 12.6 million to 4.7 million nationally within one decade.[9] In 2006, Congress reauthorized the reform by embracing work-first even more enthusiastically. This was perhaps the most successful social program in generations. (As this is being written, Congress is considering their reauthorization with stronger work requirements and less education and training.)

Welfare reform's success has been widely acknowledged. However, far less widely acknowledged is that the nation still has a tremendous work problem. In 2013, the most recent year for which we have census data, a full 66 percent of poor people older than fifteen did not work—a total of 21 million individuals.[10] That is not just a consequence of the economic crisis: in 2007, pre-crash, the number was 16 million individuals, or 64 percent of poor people older than fifteen.[11] Nor does it imply a situation in which one parent works while the other raises the kids, since in 2013, 42 percent of all poor families had no working members at all.[12] Though welfare reform succeeded in getting many poor people into jobs and reducing the welfare rolls by over two-thirds,[13] millions remain on welfare and security net assistance such as Medicaid, public housing, Food Stamps, and disability payments.

My experience with long-term dependency has led me to propose a radical solution: that we abolish *all* cash welfare, as well as food and housing assistance—except for the elderly and the physically and mentally disabled—in order to move from a dependency culture to one of full employment.

What do I mean by welfare? The term used to refer to cash programs like Aid For Dependent Children (AFDC), which morphed under President Clinton to Temporary Assistance for Needy Families (TANF). Significantly TANF required that all able-bodied recipients must work to receive benefits. But it failed in some ways to eliminate unnecessary dependence. Throughout this book, when I talk of welfare generally, I am referring to all forms of public assistance. With the exception of the Earned Income Tax Credit and some other miscellaneous tax credits, which work fundamentally differently than traditional welfare, I am otherwise including food support, housing aid, day care, and the plethora of government largesse not requiring work as a mutual responsibility of our citizens.

The federal government would use the huge savings from eliminating all of these forms of welfare to create or subsidize private-sector jobs, sending money to companies to reduce the cost of hiring and paying new workers. As a last resort, the government could also create programs similar to those run by the Depression-era Works Progress Administration, paying workers to build parks, refurbish bridges, clean streets, and so forth. The workers' wages would pay for the basics—food, clothing, and shelter. I believe even conservatives, generally against public jobs, would prefer to put people to work, instead of leaving them sitting at home collecting a dole. These would be temporary jobs, and workers would transition to private-sector jobs (with the help of organizations like America Works) as they became available.

This recommendation may sound impractical. But the work-first principle can be easily implemented, even in a depressed economy. After all, despite the economic downturn, millions of jobs go unfilled every year in the United States. In September 2014, for example, the unemployment rate was at 5.9 percent, yet there were 4.7 million job openings in the United States.[14]

Jobs can't replace all welfare and poverty programs. There will always be some people who are emotionally or physically unable to work and who require government assistance. But even the deserving dependents should be more carefully scrutinized. From 2002 to 2012, the number of SSDI recipients, a federal benefits program that provides aid to disabled people unable to work, rose by 59 percent.[15] That suggests rampant abuse of the system. This is especially notable considering SSDI today costs the federal government about as much (when including its Medicare costs) as public housing, food and nutrition assistance, the school-lunch program, and cash welfare for non-disabled families combined.

In public policy, we should deduce our theory from practice. Unfortunately, most people in the business of helping the poor turn that principle upside down, proposing theories first and then basing programs on them. They will surely oppose my proposal, fleshed out in detail at the end of this book. Can we finally confront the problem of entrenched poverty and dependency and make the difficult choices necessary to fix them? The cynic in me sees little chance that the elites who drive public policy would seriously consider my proposals. However, if the public only knew how the game was rigged, they would likely heartily approve. My optimistic side, the one shaped by finding jobs for thousands of supposedly unemployable welfare recipients, holds out hope that the nation's fiscal crisis will allow serious consideration of policies that were once unthinkable.

## Notes

1. Edward A. Suchman, *Evaluative Research: Principles and Practices in Public Service and Social Action Programs* (New York: Russell Sage, 1967), chs. 8–9.

2. U.S. Department of Commerce, Bureau of the Census, *Income and Poverty in the United States: 2013*, Series P-60, No. 249 (Washington, DC: U.S. Government Printing Office, September 2014), table B-1; http://www.heritage.org/research/reports/2014/09/the-war-on-poverty-after-50-years.

3. Lawrence M. Mead, *Government Matters: Welfare Reform in Wisconsin* (Princeton, NJ: Princeton University Press, 2004), chap. 2.

4. Calculated by averaging starting wages for all America Works job placements over calendar year 2015.

5. Vendorstat Report – Human Resources Administration. Jan. 2015. Raw data. New York.

6. M. Ann Hill, Robert Kaestner, and Thomas Main, *A Preliminary Evaluation of Welfare-to-Work Programs in New York City* (New York: Baruch College, School of Public Affairs, n.d.); Andrew R. Feldman, *What Works in Work-First Welfare: Designing and Managing Employment Programs in New York City* (Kalamazoo, MI: Upjohn Institute for Employment Research, 2011)

7. E. J. McMahon, *Trends in Assistance and Dependency: Tracking Programs for New York City's Poor, 1956–2014*. Rep. no. 86. May ed. (New York: Manhattan Institute, 2014). Print. Civic Report.

8. Keith Rockwell, "Washington: 'Let Them Eat Cake,'" *Journal of Commerce*, Sept 28, 1995, http://www.joc.com/washington-let-them-eat-cake_19950928.html.

9.   U.S. Administration for Children and Families, *Temporary Assistance for Needy Families Program: Tenth Report to Congress* (Washington, DC: U.S. Administration for Families and Children, n.d.), Appendix Table 2.1.

10.  U.S. Bureau of the Census, March 2014 Current Population Survey, table POV22.

11.  U.S. Bureau of the Census, March 2008 Current Population Survey, table POV22.

12.  U.S. Bureau of the Census, March 2014 Current Population Survey, table POV06.

13.  From their height in fiscal 1994, the AFDC/TANF rolls dropped by 68 percent through 2000. See S. Administration for Children and Families, *Temporary Assistance for Needy Families Program: Tenth Report to Congress* (Washington, DC: U.S. Administration for Families and Children, n.d.), Appendix Table 2.1.

14.  "Databases, Tables & Calculators by Subject." *Bureau of Labor Statistics Data*. United States Department of Labor, n.d. Web. 09 Aug. 2016.

15.  U.S. Social Security Administration, *Annual Statistical Yearbook, 2013* (Washington, DC: U.S. Social Security Administration, February 2014), appendix table 5.A17.

# 1

# The War on Poverty Begins: Benevolence Balloons

*"Benevolence is the heroin of the Enlightened"*
—David Stove[1]

Few, except those who were directly involved, remember the hope and enthusiasm that accompanied the early days of the War on Poverty. In the early 1960s, the feeling was almost that of a revolution, the shared sense of purpose intoxicating—we who were involved quickly became comrades-in-arms while fighting a common enemy. The Civil Rights Movement was in full throttle as Martin Luther King, Jr. led marches and made speeches encouraging our country to fulfill its promise of equality for all. The country was in the midst of great change and it was one of those epochal transformations that alerted me to my true purpose in life.

I was driving to the University of Wisconsin-Madison for a graduate sociology class when the raw and frigid day was shattered by a report over the radio that President John F. Kennedy had been shot. The announcer promised more details in a moment, and then switched over to a report on hog futures on the Chicago Mercantile Exchange. My jaw dropped. Our president was dying, and here I was in a place that was equating the tragedy with the prices of pork.

I had always known that I wanted to work for the common good, to help achieve the dreams as described by Kennedy and King and others before them. However, up until that moment, I had allowed complacency to guide my course in life. Having done well as an undergraduate in sociology, I took the scholarship offered to me in that discipline and headed to Wisconsin. I was training to be a teacher or researcher, even though neither field fit my interests or my talents. My ill-informed decision to go to graduate school in sociology had ignored my activist bent.

I had grown up in Massachusetts in a liberal Jewish household. Born in 1940, the first time I saw my parents cry was when President Roosevelt died. They voted for Henry A. Wallace, a liberal politician and the Progressive Party candidate in the 1948 presidential election. I learned the vileness of racism and was taught to avoid prejudice. I was counseled to question authority, know right, wrong, and truth when I saw them, and always challenge common wisdom. The Talmudic process for coming to a sensible answer permeated my upbringing. Perhaps it is no accident then that to this day my mantra for living is Rabbi Abraham Joshua Heschel's admonition, "See not what you know, know what you see."

During his all-too-brief presidency, John F. Kennedy signaled that he wanted to reform the nation's Depression-era welfare system by giving "a hand up, not a handout" to the poor. As political and social scientist Charles Murray noted in his 1984 magisterial study *Losing Ground*, Kennedy's small initiative, which "consisted of a few training programs and other rehabilitative efforts amounting to only $59 million in the 1963 budget, . . . . represented a major departure nonetheless," since it shifted welfare policy "away from the dole and toward escape from the dole." When President Lyndon

B. Johnson expanded Kennedy's program into the War on Poverty, he likewise hoped not to mire generations in dependency but to free them from it. "The days of the dole in this country are numbered," Johnson promised at the signing ceremony for the War on Poverty legislation in August 1964.

By 1965 I had become one of the many thousands, perhaps millions—including future President Bill Clinton—who were drawn to public service. We were on the front lines of a righteous war, and we believed we were going to prevail. The Cuban missile crisis and the awareness each day that the Cold War could bring about global nuclear annihilation had us all pessimistic about the world's future. And along had come a president who gave us hope and called us to action. Then he was gone. That we could be benevolent in his name at a time when assassinations were prevalent (in only a five more years, we'd witness the deaths of two other great fighters, Robert F. Kennedy and Martin Luther King, Jr.) was a tonic of huge potency.

The idealism of "We Shall Overcome" and "Blowing in the Wind" was everywhere. My friends and other young people were consumed with the struggles and rewards of fighting injustice and poverty. I know this is hard to believe, but we could not wait for the next LP by a folk singer—Phil Ochs, Dylan, Pete Seeger—or a rock group—Crosby Stills Nash and Young, or Big Brother and The Holding Company with Janis Joplin—to be called to arms and recommit to a cause. I was there at Woodstock, and if you wanted sentimentality, it was there to be found in all its rain-soaked, muddy, drug-infused glory. We were going to change the world and at that point in my passage no cynicism was going to trump our mission.

Yet now I see, in our youthful ignorance, the passion of my cohort's mission befogged our thinking of how to effectively wage War on Poverty and injustice.

There were two sides to the new energy pervading the era. In Kenneth Minogue's introduction to his 1963 classic, *The Liberal Mind*, he states that "the young and the radical in the Western World were in a restive condition. The restiveness had two sides, one cynical, the other sentimental. The cynical side was irresistibly seductive. It was immediately conspicuous in the satire boom, in which parodists such as Tom Lehrer, Mort Sahl, and Lenny Bruce mocked censorship, respectability, prudery, the rule of old men, and the burdens laid upon us by the past." I owned all of their records and, like so many others, quite willingly fell into the company of the cynical.

Sticking it to the establishment was heroic, and humor was a tame but safe way of expressing our dissatisfaction. Questioning and criticism were admired. Adherence to tradition was not. As Minogue continues in his own defense: "I loved all of this, not wisely but too well . . . . What I did not immediately realize was that a political program which consisted simply of thumbing one's nose at the pomposities of the Establishment would devastate what we may, as a shorthand, call culture and morality. . . . All can be destroyed when derision becomes formularized. . . . The politics of the liberal mind is a melodrama of oppressors and victims."[2]

It was at this intersection of cynicism and sentimentality that I found myself when I graduated from college and began my search for the mission that led me to become a social activist. Sentimentality led to my becoming a true believer. But it was my cynicism that ultimately pushed me to abandon these policies, reject sentimentality, and forge a more realistic and effective instrument for reducing poverty.

By the mid-1960s, America was the world's most affluent society, and economists predicted that the economic boom and high employment rates would continue for many years to come. The "conquest of poverty," the 1964 Economic Report of the president explained, was "well within our power. About $11 billion a year would bring all poor families up to the $3,000 income level we have taken to be the minimum for a decent life."[3, 4] The following year, the government allocated even more than the report had called for—$14.7 billion. "The majority of the Nation could simply tax themselves enough to provide the necessary income supplements to their less fortunate citizens."

That money deployed an arsenal of supposedly innovative weapons, including Community Action Agencies requiring "maximum feasible participation"—a policy requiring that the poor themselves should be involved as much as possible in the planning and execution of poverty programs. Social policy elites and the media jumped onto the bandwagon, predicting that the war would finally overcome the structural poverty imposed by the existing economic order. This might be from a lack of jobs or low paying ones. Our understanding of the poverty, that it was the result of society's faults, rather than an individual's failings, had been bolstered by the success of Michael Harrington's 1962 book *The Other America*, the hugely influential study of the egregious conditions of America's underclass, as well as John Kenneth Galbraith's *The Affluent Society*, which reputedly influenced the thinking of JFK and his advisers.[5]

It was in this optimistic political and ideological atmosphere that I became a young antipoverty warrior, arriving in New York City in 1965 to work for the Anti-Poverty Operations Board, a new agency created by Mayor Robert Wagner to manage the city's cut of federal War on Poverty funding. One of my first assignments was to help write the city's funding proposal to the federal government. I recall going to City Hall at 3 AM one day, getting deputy mayor Julius C. C. Edelstein's signature on that proposal, and then racing to LaGuardia Airport for the Eastern Airlines shuttle to Washington, DC, so that I could deliver the document to the Office of Economic Opportunity just ahead of the official deadline.

Through the first few years of the program, I worked for the city with other young liberal policy analysts, making decisions about which local antipoverty groups deserved federal funding. It's almost impossible to describe the excitement we felt as we crafted plans for new programs. Designed with very few budget constraints, the programs earmarked federal funding for health care, education and training, housing assistance, counseling, and other social services. They were meant to prepare the poor for their new social responsibilities and supply the assistance necessary to become self-sufficient. Inspired partly by our slain president, who had challenged us to ask what we could do for our country, and partly by our belief that the cold and aloof economic system needed to be humanized by compassionate social justice policies, we believed that we were part of something great and good.

But the government's unprecedented expenditures failed to bring about the decline in poverty that Johnson had promised. Instead, they made things worse. At the time, we did not know what was working and what wasn't, considering how many bad proposals were approved in such a short time. Yet even in the face of failure, my enthusiasm was undiminished; I had become a true believer. Along with my colleagues on the left, I continued to think that income transfers, social services, and a reliance on improving human capital were the most effective way to reduce the human pain of poverty. This was grounded in my belief that capitalism was in large part the cause of continued poverty in America, and those receiving aid were marginalized by an unfeeling system through no fault of their own.

These beliefs gradually began to erode. The education and training programs we operated weren't reducing the welfare rolls, and being reliant on government handouts was just as clearly not improving the quality of life of America's poor. It could have been argued at the time that those organizations charged with executing poverty programs were not up to the task, due to poor leadership and planning. But we idealistic antipoverty warriors knew though that our operations were generally well run, and nevertheless they failed just the same. As the years went by, I became less and less enamored with the liberal approach to reducing poverty.

The Community Action Agency, created by the Economic Opportunity Act in 1964 as the flagship of the national War on Poverty, was supposed to assure "maximum feasible participation" by the poor themselves in the running of antipoverty efforts.[6] What has not been acknowledged by scholars and others is the corrosive effect of civil rights tactics as applied on the ground to poverty programs and their funding. In many cases, policy-makers and program administrators distributed funds directly to former Civil Rights Movement organizers and other community activists, which were then funneled to incompetent organizations unable to deliver quality programs. In the same spirit that informed the Watergate investigation, if you wish to know why Head Start and other programs failed, follow the money.

It didn't take long for these programs' inherent issues to reveal themselves. In 1967 I was an official reviewing proposals for funding in New York City. Community groups were asked to write these proposals detailing what they would do with the money and how much it would cost. We attracted groups hoping to set up neighborhood health clinics, early childhood education, job training programs, English as a second-language classes, and so on. I remember one day when I was working at my desk near City Hall when the door of my office flew open and I heard a man shout, "Are you Peter Cove?" It was Major Owens, previously a civil rights activist,

now a community organizer, and later to become a Congressman. Owens was leading a group of activists demanding
funding for their projects. We had considered and formally
rejected their proposals, and now they had arrived to conduct
a sit-in in protest.

I attempted to reason with the group. I told them that
they had lost to other more worthy groups. This attempt
at an explanation did not satisfy them. They were trying to
shake me down and, truthfully, I was a bit scared. We think
of civil rights activities as nonviolent but in the late 1960s
activism had begun to assume a more muscular and intim-
idating character. Here I was with a group of angry activists
openly threatening me and blocking me from exiting. After
some heated discussions and even suggestions of violence,
I told them to "go fuck themselves," straight-armed my way
out, and left them sitting on my office floor. They were not
there the next morning.

My experience was repeated in many offices in New York
and around the country. Organizations took advantage of
maximum feasible participation to shakedown politicians
and bureaucrats for more and more funding. As civil rights
activities subsided in the South after the passage of the Civil
Rights Act (1964) and the Voting Rights Act (1965), many
involved with those successes were redirecting their attention
to the poverty program. Federal funding was just beginning,
and community action, through "maximum feasible participation" (the involvement of the poor to create and run
new poverty programs), was creating a whole new arena for
demands, control, and "sticking it to the man."

Fred Siegel, an eminent historian and social commentator (full disclosure: he is also a close friend and advisor),
has helped me to understand precisely what transpired. He
observed that the Black Power Movement could also be
described as the black patronage movement. Money was

poured into black organization as reparations for past mis-
deeds and, more cynically, as building blocks for bringing
out the increasingly organized black vote. The efficacy of
these monies ceased to be at issue. Job training dollars, for
instance, rarely prepared people for better paying jobs and
turned into racial entitlement. According to Siegel's history
of the era, "By the spring and summer of 1968, sit-ins at city
welfare centers and at [welfare commissioner] Ginsberg's
office brought both chaos and an increase in special grant
money. . . . By fall of 1968 the protests swelled to more than
two hundred incidents a month. The overwhelmed welfare
department had to establish a war room to keep track of the
daily actions, as demonstrators ripped phones from the walls
and trashed welfare offices."

It's important to be clear that I am not suggesting a racial
element by teasing out the connection between welfare, the
techniques of the civil rights movement, and poverty in this
way. When the War on Poverty started, we young crusad-
ers set forth to stamp out poverty universally—and poverty
certainly crossed racial lines: 2.3 million white people lived
underneath the poverty line at the time, while 1.05 million
non-white people suffered the same fate. We set out to help
*all* of them—however, the application of the tools of the civil
rights movement to the administration of poverty programs
set us on the course for disaster.[7]

Soon the War on Poverty became transactional: politicians
awarded lucrative contracts to questionable programs in
exchange for votes. This corruption was already spreading as
early as January of 1969—according to Siegel, in that month
"the *Times* broke a major scandal with this headline: Millions
In City Poverty Agency Lost By Fraud And Inefficiency. A
group of social service administrative staff employees, the
so-called Durham gang, had rigged the computer to write
checks for imaginary workers." Although the sit-ins and

direct actions have ceased, that same climate of corruption remains today.[8]

The reality is that this corruption was baked in from the start. In *Launching the War on Poverty*, Michael Gillette recounts oral histories of some of the planners. There was deliberate thought that went into assuring that community action would allow for, and even encourage, fighting city hall. In the planners' discussions we begin to see how the establishment of parallel political operations constituted a new form of patronage and cronyism.[9]

Clear from the oral histories is the fact that, for some, bypassing local authority was a desirable and a specific goal. For some others, confrontation might be inevitable. But they all underestimated the effects of society's recent experience with civil disobedience and the mistrust of authority. The communities to be served were often coterminous with civil rights activity and the community leaders were well schooled in their tactics and eager to apply them to this new war. Such techniques might be appropriate for civil rights, but not so for fighting poverty.[10]

The idea of maximum feasible participation was born out of this residual mistrust of authority. War on Poverty organizers believed that poor people knew what they needed to pull themselves up from want. Further, they could best plan and operate the programs that would effectuate their release from impoverishment, not the government. The resulting concept was maximum feasible participation, which proved to be a false hope based on no proven theory whatsoever. The resulting headlong rush to deliver money to poor communities resulted in poor programs. It was Dick Boone working with the planning group for the war who defined and pushed for maximum feasible participation. From Nicholas Lemann's 1991 book *The Promised Land*, here is the backstory of how the ill-formed and failed strategy was created:

Boone didn't know exactly how maximum feasible participation would work when it was put into practice, and the uncertainty was part of the appeal. He liked to think of himself as a light-spirited, adventurous government official—liked, as he puts it, "just shaking things up." The highest accolade he can bestow on something he has done is to say, "That was fun." Pushing maximum feasible participation was fun. It might mean simply soliciting poor people as to their needs. It might be a way of funneling the social service jobs the poverty program would create to poor people instead of civil servants and social workers. It might, in the Chicago reform spirit, be a way of wresting control of a government entity from the machine. It might create some action in local elective politics. As Boone says, "It might lead somewhere, but we didn't know where."

Finally, the idea almost accidentally takes over:

Boone's concept of maximum feasible participation sounded like a minor point not worth arguing over at length. On Tuesday, February 4, the third day of the meetings, as Yarmolinsky remembered it, "Dick Boone kept bringing up the idea of maximum feasible participation. Whether he used those words then I don't recall. I said to Dick, 'You've brought that idea up several times,' and he said, 'Yes, I have. How many more times do I have to bring it up before it gets into the program?' And I said, 'Oh, two or three.' He did, and it did." Like supply-side economics in the 1980s, maximum feasible participation was a new and untested idea that, because it happened to hit Washington at a propitious moment, overnight became a sweeping national policy.[11]

Lyndon Johnson and his top aides were almost unconsciously melding the tactics and strategies of civil rights activists with sweeping government policy. Yet they were not fighting morally corrupt segregation laws, as protestors were in the South; they were fighting poverty, a result of economic and cultural forces. This melding was one of the primary reasons for the war's failure.

Yet the War on Poverty's founders and adherents were not solely to blame. The War on Poverty would have been impossible without the aid of private institutions with large amounts of money. This is why it is vital to understand the emerging activist role of foundations in American social programs.

In the words of scholar Alice O'Conner, "From their very beginnings in the early twentieth century, the 'big foundations' such as Rockefeller and Carnegie had been claiming to serve the 'general welfare' in their efforts to cultivate and mobilize scientific expertise on policy matters ranging from industrial relations, public health, and agricultural modernization to the organization of government itself. . . . By mutual agreement, the foundations would do what, as Stanley Katz and Barry Karl put it, government '*did not, or could not, or should not do.*'"[12]

Early on in their development, foundations were cautious about the power they wielded. In sociologist Gunner Myrdal's landmark study of race relations, *An American Dilemma*, commissioned by the Carnegie Foundation, the president of the foundation provided an introduction to the book that gives a sense of how foundations initially saw their role. "Provided the foundation limits itself to its proper function, namely, to make the facts available and then let them speak for themselves, and does not undertake to instruct the public as to what to do about them, studies of this kind provide a wholly proper and . . . sometimes a highly important use of [its] funds."[13] Yet in time, the foundations would grow far more activist in their strategies.

The largest of the new wave of foundations, the Ford Foundation, was endowed with $500 million in assets from the Ford Motor Company in 1950 and began working for educational reform, the advancement of the social sciences, and the improvement of race relations. The programs that the Ford Foundation funded, particularly its Fund for the Advancement of Education and Mobilization for Youth, were direct predecessors and models for the community action programs that would characterize the War on Poverty.[14] The ongoing connection between foundation activities and government policy became apparent to me while working for the New World Foundation in New York City in 1970. The New World Foundation had been hugely instrumental in helping finance civil rights activities in the South, particularly the Southern Christian Leadership Conference, the civil rights organization whose first president was Martin Luther King, Jr. This strategy of supporting community action not only supplied needed funds, but granted further legitimacy to grassroots efforts. Other foundations, such as the Stern Family Fund and the Field Foundation, followed a similar path in allocating their resources.

The Ford Foundation was at the center of this new foundation-funded activism. Helped by tax exemptions, foundations across America had marshaled enormous amounts of private, philanthropic money to put toward influencing public policy. However, by the mid-1950s, the climate of McCarthyism and suspicion led congressmen to investigate the finances of these liberal foundations. Foundations presidents grew increasingly worried that the government would shut them down if they couldn't demonstrate their value as incubators of useful, effective government policy. As the newest, and largest, of the foundations, the Ford Foundation decided to try something new. Thus the Gray Areas Project was born.[15]

Led by social theorist Paul Ylvisaker, Gray Areas targeted urban poverty and sought to craft new policies and programs

that the government could put into action. Scholar Heather
Mac Donald pulls out one telling quote of Ylvisaker that
reveals how much more activist the self-image of the foundation was becoming—he stated that the role of foundations
should be to point out "programs and policies, such as social
security, income maintenance, and educational entitlement
that convert isolated and discretionary acts of private charity
into regularized public remedies that flow as a matter of leg-
islated right." The foundation measured the success of Gray
Areas by the number of federal visitors to the program's sites,
and it declared the passage of the Economic Opportunity
Act of 1964, which inaugurated the War on Poverty and
incorporated the Ford-invented community action agencies,
to be Gray Areas' "proudest achievement." Gray Areas ended
up becoming the template for all that the War on Poverty
would become.[16]

From the Gray Areas Project to the financing of intermediaries to run and research poverty programs, Ford led the
march for America's foundations to become active participants in rearranging local political systems by empowering
Community Action Agencies to operate and fight against
perceived grievances. Their new role marked a seismic shift
toward antiestablishment support. It would fit right in with
the civil rights movement and the civil disturbances of the
1960s.

Important here is the recognition that a liberal perspective
on how poverty grew and why it did was fundamental to the
War on Poverty from the very beginning. It was predicated
on the belief that society, not individuals, caused poverty. Personal responsibility took a back seat to victimization. I knew
many of the people at Ford responsible for poverty policy. I
also knew many who ran the programs they supported. I ran
some of these myself. Later on I observed those responsible
for evaluating their programs. Biased liberal economists, such

as those populating the board of Manpower Demonstration Research Corporation, and, yes, even previously committed Communists such as my old (now deceased) friend Robert Schrank populated the higher ranks of their leadership.

Ironically, though many of the foundations were built from the wealth of industrialists, they held a distinct antibusiness bias and the programs acted on it. This may represent a more general tendency the foundations had toward being anti-status quo, regardless of the policy implications or social ramifications. To be sure, something needed to change to assuage urban poverty, but the foundations' targets were not always well chosen. Following Ford's foray into activist and antiestablishment territory, it mounted a campaign for community schools. This amounted to an attack on the legitimacy of existing institutions, in this case public education's way of doing business. It made no strides toward creating better schools and resulted only in inciting community disruption and violent protests. Instead of working to strengthen the role and delivery of the schools, a parallel and competing battalion of disgruntled parents and community organizers were charged with creating local school boards and programs. As an ivory tower proposition, this sounded pretty good in theory. But as with community action, Head Start, and the maximum feasible participation aspect of the poverty programs, it ultimately failed in the field. Few if any of the original foundation-supported antipoverty programs could show that they actually reduced poverty.[17]

About five years after the start of the national poverty program I too went to work for a foundation. The New World Foundation in New York had been established by another successful industrialist, Cyrus McCormick, the founder of International Harvester. As a pro-business capitalist Henry Ford would have done had he lived to observe the funding patterns of his foundation in the 1960s and 1970s, old Cyrus must have been rolling in his grave considering what New World ended up funding.

In keeping with the tenor of the times, New World had become stridently liberal, behaving as if its very purpose was to attack the established civil order and institutions. In the case of civil rights, it pioneered good and useful programs. However, many of their projects sadly aped the ongoing civil disobedience, youth sentiment, and hippie culture prevalent at the time, and I willingly fell in line. For instance, the Rockefeller Foundation was at that time funding Saul Alinsky's Industrial Areas Foundation in Chicago. Alinsky was the father of community organization and focused on educating a cadre of people skilled in challenging authority and existing institutions. No question, there was much about society at the time that rightfully needed to be changed—I spent time in the South helping some worthy civil rights groups gain the financial support to get racist laws changed. But that was a fight against systematic and at the time legal prejudice. The same tactics used by Dr. King and others to attack racism were disastrously misplaced when applied to the War on Poverty, since poverty was not a deliberate act of societal injustice but a result of complex economic and cultural factors. The strategies for change implemented by the civil rights movement were superimposed on the problems of poverty. Foundations unfortunately fell reflexively for the fight-the-man fervor of the antisegregation movements, leading those who had successfully practiced civil disobedience to misapply that tactic to ending poverty. Many of us, new social activists, bought into this antiestablishment strategy as well and adopted similar tactics ultimately to derail antipoverty efforts.

Ford Foundation's Gray Areas Project and another Ford-supported program, Mobilization for Youth, were key to spurring the poverty planners in the federal government to mount antiestablishment attacks on the problems of need and want. The architects of these programs designed the strategy of maximum feasible participation, concocted the policy prescriptions, and laid the groundwork for many of the programs that the Economic Opportunity Act of 1964 would authorize and fund on a national level. Their approach was certainly seductive—I was then an avid believer in their plans of sidestepping governors and city halls and empowering poor people directly. Power to the people, they believed. Yet this had the unfortunate result of trading program effectiveness for community control. Some programs had the potential to be truly effective. But the tendency to devolve program control to a willing reservoir of civil rights activists and community leaders as previously cited tended to subvert even the best conceived programs.

Head Start, a preschool education program aimed at disadvantaged children and one of the ballyhooed programs of the War on Poverty, is a telling example. There is every reason to believe early childhood education can make a difference. But look at its results. According to the government's own research, most benefits gained from Head Start are lost after the first year out.[18] Why? Because the programs were run by community activists who cared more for the buoyancy of their organizations than the quality of services they were being paid to deliver. Even after the War on Poverty officially ended with the abolition of the Office of Economic Opportunity, money continued to flow from DC to cities and states for many programs aimed at a reduction in poverty. However, the game had morphed into the same or similar organizations receiving public support from politicians in exchange for money and votes. With maximum feasible participation no longer in play, and with city halls now back in control, money flowed to the organizations that delivered political support. The irony is that many of the same groups fighting city hall were now in bed with those politicians that would siphon money to their organizations. The public protests ended, replaced by backroom deals.

At the time I was a formidable antiestablishment advocate, and my programs reflected this. It did not occur to me then that this ought to have been a revolution of intent, to help those in need, not a revolution to bring legitimate institutions to their knees. Over time, our liberal ideals were to become the victims of untested policies and naive government intervention. Our benevolent actions went haywire and hurt the very ones we were trying to help.

The War on Poverty officially began with a $1 billion appropriation in 1964 and spent another $2 billion in the following two years. This and other legislation spawned dozens of programs, among them are

- the Job Corps, whose purpose was to help disadvantaged youth develop marketable skills;
- the Neighborhood Youth Corps, established to give poor urban youth work experience and to encourage them to stay in school;
- Volunteers in Service to America (VISTA), a domestic version of the Peace Corps, which placed concerned citizens with community-based agencies to work toward empowerment of the poor;
- the Model Cities Program, which developed new antipoverty programs and urban development projects through coordination between the Department of Housing and Urban Development and local urban leaders;
- Upward Bound, which assisted poor high school students entering college;
- legal services for the poor;
- the Food Stamp Act of 1964 (which expanded the federal food stamp program);
- the Community Action Program, which initiated local Community Action Agencies charged with helping the poor become self-sufficient;
- Project Head Start, which offered preschool education for poor children.[19]

In addition, funding was provided for the establishment of community health centers to expand access to health care, while major amendments were made to Social Security in 1965 and 1967, which significantly increased benefits, expanded coverage, and established new programs to combat poverty and raise living standards. In addition, average Aid to Families with Dependent Children (AFDC) payments, set by states, was 35 percent higher in 1968 than in 1960, but remained insufficient and uneven.

The popularity of the War on Poverty waned after the 1960s. The Office of Economic Opportunity was dismantled by President Nixon in 1973, although many of the programs were transferred to other government agencies. Deregulation, growing criticism of the welfare state, and an ideological shift to conservatism in the 1980s and 1990s culminated in the Personal Responsibility and Work Opportunity Act of 1996, which, in the words of its champion President Clinton, "end[ed] welfare as we know it."

In the year that I joined the War on Poverty, 1965, the poverty rate was 17.3 percent in the United States. In 2013 it was 14.5 percent, and we had spent in over $22 trillion to obtain this small improvement![20] This cannot be blamed purely on program failure—with such an enormous outlay of money one would have expected more. This did not happen.

Charles Murray, in his seminal work *Losing Ground*, meticulously took his readers through the failures of the War on Poverty and backed up his assertions with statistics to prove their legitimacy. I saw this failure happen in real time though I was slow to recognize it. As years went on, I saw more and more women heading families with no father in sight. And we all knew the father was hiding when the social workers made house calls to certify the woman's eligibility for continued support. If the lie was uncovered, the welfare recipient's support would be canceled since—with a man around—the laws assumed that she had a means of support. (Today, there are still few fathers in sight, but unfortunately this time they aren't just hiding in the closet.)[21] The use of drugs by welfare recipients also increased, as did family dysfunction. One needs only to look at pictures of the blight in the Bronx in the 1970s to begin to understand what our welfare policies were accomplishing—an erosion of community and families. The number of reported heroin users in New York City between the years 1964 and 1967 nearly tripled from sixty-five thousand to one hundred and forty-five thousand reported users between 1971 and 1974.[22]

In 1973 when I began working with welfare recipients in a significant way, I was part of the National Supported Work Demonstration operated by MDRC. They directed each program across the country to work with those perceived to be the hardest to employ. A welfare recipient had to have been on welfare for thirty of the last thirty-six months to qualify. The assumption was that their longevity on welfare meant that they must be among the most difficult to employ. But this was not actually the case. We found that the older enrollees had actually gone to better public schools than the more recent ones. They had experience running a family and budgeting their money. In fact, the inside joke of the program operators was "Throw us into the briar patch!"—we were delighted to have the chance to work with these supposedly unemployable clients. As the years passed, the newer welfare participants tended to be younger, multigenerational dependents, worse-educated, and mired in mindsets that defined a growing culture of accepted dependency.

And fatherless families had become the rule. In 1969, 43 percent of welfare children received aid because their mother was divorced or separated from the father, and 28 percent because she was never married to him. By 1995, the comparable figures were 25 and 57 percent—more than a reversal.[23] Fatherless children are more prone to bad outcomes such as crime, drug use, school dropouts, and their own out of wedlock births than are children raised by both parents—even controlling for other influences such as income or education.[24] Because of welfare policies and those of the War on Poverty, a culture was being created that encouraged absent fathers. This would push the rolls upward in startling numbers until welfare reform was finally passed in the 1990s.

I should probably note here, that while I do describe the changes in the demographics of the people on welfare, the cause for increased dependency is not due solely to the characteristics of the dependents themselves. The increase has to be assigned as well to the government's policies. The simple fact is there are more subsidies for remaining dependent and their proliferation—that is, Food Stamps, SSDI, Welfare without work, Housing allowances, and the rest—makes welfare the more financially sound choice. There is ample evidence, for instance, that many people maxing out their five years on welfare have routinely applied for and been granted SSDI. Here we have had a move from one dependency to another. I believe everyone is employable, regardless of the demographic or their perceived barrier. But faced with a choice of significant government assistance or work, that choice becomes harder.

The War on Poverty, though begun in earnest, has turned into a war on the poor themselves. I was there. I believed we had a calling that was noble and right. I wish that I had then the knowledge and perception to understand that we were creating the forces that would perpetuate and increase dependency. Only now, through the prism of time, do I understand why the war failed.

The programs I cut my teeth on in the mid-1960s unknowingly caused this increase in dependency while trying to alleviate poverty. Again, programs focused on "maximum feasible participation" played an outsized role by encouraging the poor to establish support structures parallel to the established polity (usually a mayor or city council) and demand help not already being provided by the state. This had the effect of increasing the supply of goods and services that ironically would keep the poor more dependent. There were two reasons for this. First, the programs themselves were run by inexperienced community organizations. City halls happily traded contracts for votes, leading to poor programs for poor people.

Head Start, the first major preschool program, was not a bad idea in and of itself. Preschool education can be important in giving children from poor neighborhoods a jump start in life. It has failed because of the general inadequacies of their deliverers. Similarly, vocational and job training activities can work. But Job Corps and Neighborhood Youth Corps, both started by OEO, failed because those put in charge did not know how to build and run the programs. This still goes on today.

Second, empowered by the Office of Economic Opportunity, demands for increases in financial and in-kind aid have only increased, stimulating a growing dependency culture. The welfare rights movement cynically encouraged more people to go on welfare and increase the benefits in order to break the system.

It is important to understand that the impetus for our current growing expansion of dependency emanates from the initial empowerment of community action in the 1960s. The interplay between community groups and the established political structures set the stage for a steady and rising flow of cash to fuel programs, regardless of their effectiveness.

I've seen first hand the perverse effect that these structures can have on policy-making. A powerful state politician in New York—responsible for the direction of statewide social welfare spending—once visited America Works. After a tour, she observed that it looked like one of the best welfare-to-work programs she had seen. Would we have her support in future? No. "You see, Mr. Cove," she said, "there is a community-based organization in my district. Their program is smaller than yours and probably not as good, but on Election Day, they bring out the votes." Politics always trumps good policy—the only thing unique in this case was how blunt this particular politician was about that fact.

A senior government official in Indiana once made a similar point during a meeting. Two of the primary factors used to evaluate welfare-to-work contract proposals, he explained, were the organization's location—local programs were prioritized—and whether the organization was friendly or hostile to the politicians then in office. It's interesting to contrast those factors to the criteria used for deciding whether or not to encourage a new company to come into town. Will it create jobs? Does it have a track record of success? Will it bring investment into our town? Those are the real questions government officials should be asking. The truth is that the measures of whether a program works in my business are impossibly flawed. I was at a meeting where we had protested a denial of funding by an agency. We explained that the tens upon tens of variables judging a program's potential for success were actually irrelevant. One official responded by saying "All you people care about is jobs!"

I have stated on many occasions that our industry, including welfare-to-work and job training programs, is the most corrupt government service in the country. I do not mean that stealing and direct payoffs happen regularly. To my knowledge they don't. What I mean is there is a conspiracy to foreswear performance for political support. So when we pushed the government to award contracts based on results rather than process, we found government officials fighting us at every juncture. Why? Paying contractors based on results would expose the good and—more likely—the bad. That information would then prevent politicians from directing contracts to ill-performing organizations in trade for their support. The game would be over.

How did we and the architects in Washington misread the situation so badly? Hindsight suggests that we were in part caught in the trap Nathan Glazer suggests is a liberal canard—"that for every social problem there is a program that can address it."[25] What seemed like good ideas at the time spawned, in fact, mostly ill-conceived or poorly run attempts at solutions. Simply this was the mismanaging of misguided solutions.

It is also clear that even LBJ was fixed on jobs as the solution. No fan of welfare, at one point, he told Bill Moyers, "You tell Shriver [one of the architects of the War on Poverty], no doles!"[26] Community action upset his sensibilities for planning and delivery of services. He had seen the Civilian Conservation Corps succeed in getting people to work during the Great Depression and he wanted his new versions—NYC, NJC, VISTA, and so forth—to help get people working. "I thought we were going to have CCC camps," Johnson said to Moyers on another occasion, " . . . and I thought we were going to have community action where a city or county or a school district or some governmental agency could sponsor a project—state highway department sponsor it—and we'd pay the labor and a very limited amount of materials on it but make them put up most of the materials and a good deal of supervision and so forth just like we used to have."[27] Unfortunately, "community action" ultimately meant maximum feasible participation, rather than locally directed sponsorship of projects. What's worse, Johnson retreated on Kennedy's strategy to create jobs through tax cuts and backed training and education programs rather than direct placement into jobs. Those programs were in turn delegated to inept community groups or civil servants incapable of delivering effective services and unprepared to place people into jobs. Johnson was right about jobs, but his weakened War on Poverty could not effectively mount a strategy to deliver them.

What's more, something had changed in American culture. As the nonviolence of the Civil Rights Movement wound down and was replaced by the more forthright militancy of the Black Power Movement, there was a growing sense among the intellectual elite that terrible crimes had been committed, such as slavery, and that society itself was to blame for poverty and any other ills that befell the downtrodden. Restitution and reparations were in order, and a culture of blame eased aside the personal responsibility ingrained in our country's DNA. Nor was this strictly about race—white activists on the left joined with black nationalists demanding a radical expansion of the welfare state, barely managing to conceal their larger goal of a much more drastic, revolutionary societal change. Powered by such attitudes, politicians were encouraged to pander to racial and radical demands for what can only be called hush money. Tom Wolfe got it right in his 1970 essay "Mau-Mauing the Flak Catchers": the liberal elite allied with the self-anointed victims to force ever more funding and services onto the oppressed. Some of this was anticapitalism, some Marxist propaganda, some honest but naive benevolence, but all of it served to expand dependence—a topic vital to understanding the decline of work, and the subject we shall turn to next.

## Notes

1. David Stove, *What's Wrong with Benevolence* (New York: Encounter Books, 2011).
2. Kenneth Minogue, *The Liberal Mind* (Indianapolis, IN: Liberty Fund, 2000), ix.
3. Factoring for inflation, that would amount to over $23,000 today.

4.    Calculated using inflation calculator on US Bureau of Labor Statistics web page, November 12, 2014.

5.    http://www.nytimes.com/2009/06/21/books/review/ Isserman-t.html?_r=0; Michael B. Katz, *The Undeserving Poor: America's Enduring Confrontation with Poverty* (New York: Oxford University Press, 2013), 104–5.

6.    Daniel P. Moynihan, *Maximum Feasible Misunderstanding: Community Action in the War on Poverty* (New York: Free Press, 1970), chaps. 5, 7.

7.    https://www.ssa.gov/policy/docs/ssb/v29n5/v29n5p3.pdf.

8.    Fred Siegel, *The Future Once Happened Here: New York, DC, LA and the Fate of America's Big Cities* (New York: Encounter Books, 2000), 63–64.

9.    Michael Gillette, *Launching the War on Poverty*, 2nd ed. (New York: Oxford University Press, 2010).

10.   Ibid., 94.

11.   Nicholas Lemann, *The Promised Land: The Great Black Migration and How It Changed America* (New York: Knopf, 1991), 152–3.

12.   O'Conner, Alice. "The Ford Foundation and Philanthropic Activism in the 1960s," in *Philanthropic Foundations: New Scholarship, New Possibilities*, ed. Ellen Condliffe Lagemann (Bloomington: Indiana University Press, 1999), 169.

13.   Heather Mac Donald, "The Billions of Dollars That Made Things Worse, *CityJournal*, Autumn 1996.

14.   Gregory K. Raynor, "The Ford Foundation's War on Poverty," in *Philanthropic Foundations: New Scholarship, New Possibilities*, ed. Ellen Condliffe Lagemann (Bloomington: Indiana University Press, 1999), 195.

15.   Alice O'Conner, "The Ford Foundation and Philanthropic Activism in the 1960s," in *Philanthropic Foundations: New Scholarship, New Possibilities*, ed. Ellen Condliffe Lagemann (Bloomington: Indiana University Press, 1999), 170.

16.   See note 32 above.

17.   Henry J. Aaron, *Politics and the Professors: The Great Society in Perspective* (Washington, DC: Brookings, 1978).

18.   U.S. Administration for Children and Families, *Head Start Impact Study: Final Report* (Washington, DC: U.S. Administration for Children and Families, January 2010).

19.  This listing comes from the Boundless web site: https://www.boundless.com/u-s-history/textbooks/boundless-u-s-history-textbook/the-sixties-1960-1969-29/the-lyndon-b-johnson-administration-223/the-war-on-poverty-1247-8801/.

20.  Poverty statistics from U.S. Department of Commerce, Bureau of the Census, *Income and Poverty in the United States: 2013*, Series P-60, No. 249 (Washington, DC: U.S. Government Printing Office, September 2014), table B-1. Spending figure from Rector and Sheffield, "The War on Poverty after Fifty Years," http://www.heritage.org/research/reports/2014/09/the-war-on-poverty-after-50-years.; Current poverty rate from https://www.census.gov/content/dam/Census/library/publications/2014/demo/p60-249.pdf.

21.  Kay Hymowitz, "Boy Trouble." *City Journal*, Autumn 2013, http://www.city-journal.org/2013/23_4_boy-trouble.html.

22.  Blanche Frank, Ph.D., "An Overview of Heroin Trends in New York City: Past, Present and Future," *The Mount Sinai Journal of Medicine* October/November 67, no. 5 & 6 (2000): 340–46. Drugpolicy.org. Drug Policy Alliance, Oct. 2000. Web. January 19, 2015.

23.  U.S. Congress, House, Committee on Ways and Means, *1998 Green Book: Background Material, and Data on Programs within the Jurisdiction of the Committee on Ways and Means* (Washington, DC: U.S. Government Printing Office, May 19, 1998), 440.

24.  Sara McLanahan and Gary Sandefur, *Growing Up With a Single Parent: What Hurts, What Helps* (Cambridge, MA: Harvard University Press, 1994).

25.  Nathan Glazer, *The Limits of Social Policy* (Cambridge, MA: Harvard University Press, 1988), 3.

26.  Nicholas Lemann, *The Promised Land: The Great Black Migration and How It Changed America* (New York: Knopf, 1991), 149.

27.  http://presidentialrecordings.rotunda.upress.virginia.edu/essays?series=WarOnPoverty#fnref37.

# 2

# Our Moral Cliff:
# The Rise of Dependency

*"The growth of government has politicized
life and weakened the nation's moral fabric."*
—James A. Dorn[1]

It's impossible to talk about work without talking about
dependency. Today we see a chorus of commenters bemoaning that ours has become a nation of takers. Forty-five percent
of Americans pay no income tax but a third of Americans
receive some sort of benefit from the federal government,
taking from a system they did not help fund. Twenty-three
percent live in households where at least one member
receives support from a major welfare program (TANF,
Food Stamps, or Supplemental Security Income). And 69
percent of all federal expenditures go to finance these and
other benefit programs.[2] We have edged toward a moral cliff
where the shame of being dependent on government aid has
been replaced by a breezy bonhomie for entitlement.

While monetary poverty has to some extent been bailed
out with cash and in-kind support by government, relative

poverty and dependence has not. So the arguments currently in fashion describing inequality have some basis in fact. The poor have become less materially poor—there are TVs, cell phones, and other accouterments of the good life—but relative inequality has grown and continues to do so. Even more troubling, work participation has declined. This is especially disturbing in a country once revered for its work ethic.[3]

The numbers are startling:

- In 1962, 11.7 percent of the US population received government assistance—cash transfers of some kind; in 2012 approximately 21 percent did.[4] (To be clear, this book opposes cash transfers that do not require work for the able-bodied, except Social Security but not exempting SSDI where a person might want or be able to work.)
- In 1983, 30 percent of the population lived in a household receiving some government benefit. In 2010, 48 percent did; 34 percent received means-tested aid—that is, aid that is restricted to households below a certain income-requirement.[5]
- In 1962, there were three million five hundred and ninety-three thousand recipients of government assistance through AFDC; by 1996, when AFDC was repealed and replaced by the Temporary Assistance for Needy Families program, twelve million six hundred and forty-five thousand people were receiving AFDC assistance.[6]
- In 1965, the federal government spent $1,625 per person on poverty programs. In 2011 that figure has risen to $14,848. The Obama administration alone has increased annual spending on welfare programs by more than $193 billion.[7]
- There are 10.1 million people receiving disability payments today, up by 1.6 million under Obama and up 55 percent from a decade ago.[8]
- Since 1965, when I started working in poverty programs, the poverty rate has gone from 15.2 percent to 14.5 percent despite having spent over $22 trillion on such programs to reduce poverty.[9]

How did we come to this?

The ever-quickening erosion of America's core values coupled with our growing expectations of government has led us precipitously toward this moral cliff. Slowly slipping away are individualism and commitment grounded in hard work, personally doing good, and the proper roles of citizens within the society. The nineteenth-century French observer Alexis de Tocqueville once described the incredible American capacity for achievement, writing, "No Americans are devoid of a yearning desire to rise . . . not only are desires boundless, but the power of satisfying them seems almost boundless, too." Our attitudes have since changed, undermining our core belief in personal industriousness and ballooning our expectations of how much the government must provide. We have moved from a commitment to serve the deserving poor to an assumption that *all* are deserving. And much of this rests at the feet of politicians trolling for votes by larding on the largesse.

Safety net programs inherently cause greater levels of dependence. By offering assistance to those in need, being a person in need becomes more desirable, and an easier state to live in. Benjamin Franklin wrote:

> I am for doing good to the poor, but I differ in opinion of the means. I think the best way of doing good to the poor, is not making them easy in poverty, but leading or driving them out of it. In my youth I travelled much, and I observed in different countries, that the more public provisions were made for the poor, the less they provided for themselves, and of course became poorer. And, on the contrary, the less was done for them, the more they did for themselves, and became richer.

Welfare programs devoid of reciprocal responsibility drive out the industriousness of the individual. They encourage individuals to become content in their position of dependency, and when others find themselves newly in a position to collect welfare, either out of laziness or out of bad luck, they too encounter the same incentives. Some will pull themselves out of poverty, but the programs by their very nature insidiously erode the character of the nation.

The safety net has become a version of the old game show *Dialing for Dollars*, where all can play and most win. I have already shown you the numbers. Over the years, dependency trends have skyrocketed. The fastest-growing sectors of dependency on government assistance (i.e., the provision of shelter, food, monetary aid, health care, education, or employment training by the government) are health, welfare, and housing. Studies done by the AARP show that more than 30 million households without a person sixty-five or older receive entitlements, and according to the Heritage Foundation, 65 million individuals who are not in the military or any government position receive entitlements. Meanwhile, since 1986, the proportion of Americans who pay no federal income tax has increased from 14.8 percent to 45 percent.[10] Under this new load, America's safety net is becoming unsustainable. Since 1965, the combined federal and state welfare spending has increased (in constant 2011 dollars) from $256 billion to $908 billion.[11]

Workforce participation spiked in the 1980s and 1990s, as more women entered the ranks and the baby boomer generation swelled the working-age population[12]; but since then, the participation rate has leveled off and then dropped over 3 percent in the last six years.[13] It is tempting to blame the poor themselves for this apparent lack of industriousness among the young and able-bodied. Yet, as I have stated, those who are taking advantage of these programs are simply reacting rationally to the rules and incentives that the government has decreed, but the game is rigged.

According to a study by former Pennsylvania State Human Service Commissioner Gary Alexander, the economic incentives of aid programs are set up in such a way that work is actually discouraged. In Pennsylvania, a woman with two children earning a gross income of $29,000 is eligible to increase her income through combined state and federal support to $57,327, equivalent to what a single mother of two earning $69,000 a year would net after taxes. If, in our example, that same mother earned $1,000 more, her net income and benefits would *drop* to $49,000 under the state programs.[14] With such disincentives in place, she will logically not work toward a merit increase or even put in a few extra hours lest she be punished several times over for her initiative.

But there are also cultural reasons for why we have become so dependent. First, we have witnessed the stigma of dependency being replaced by a culture of selfishness. There was a time when being on welfare was considered shameful. There was a time when single parenthood was an embarrassment. Once, rewards for not working were ignoble. Now motherhood by women who cannot afford it or who are unemployed is considered a right that should be subsidized by the government. America now relies on SSDI and disability payouts to support an otherwise largely employable class. The life of responsibility has become like the old 1950's TV show, The Life of Riley, with most expecting government to be its underwriter in perpetuity.

The second reason, as Nathan Glazer has mentioned in his book, *The Limits of Social Policy*, is the liberal notion that every social problem must be met with government programs. And where has that gotten us? A plethora of ineffective poverty and income support programs that, despite spending more than $19 trillion since 1965, have resulted in a de minimis reduction in poverty. With that has come a staggering increase in dependency. And it is this dependency, on medical support, social security, and welfare programs, that is pushing us over the moral cliff.

How strikingly different America looked at its inception than it does today. At the time of the founding, this country was a model of unbounded opportunity. Those who wanted to work found it or created it and did not look for support from the government. The historical rise in dependence is directly correlated to the expansion of government. As the government increases in scope, it influences more areas of society and more individuals. Whether it is a regulation forcing openness in business transactions, or assistance to the poor, people then become dependent on the government for either information or payments. The gradual expansion of government reach has thus led to a gradual expansion of dependency. And, as Arthur Brooks has observed, resulted in a partial usurpation of civil society by government.

Rahm Emanuel, the current mayor of Chicago and former White House Chief of Staff under President Obama, once infamously stated, "You never want a serious crisis to go to waste. . . . This crisis [referring to the economic crisis that began in the fall of 2008] provides the opportunity for us to do things that you could not do before."[15] What is true of government today has been true throughout American history. Crises have always been a major vehicle for increasing government power. Events such as the Great Depression provided excellent opportunities for growing government action and accumulated power. Once the crisis subsides, however, there never seems to be a corresponding ratcheting down of the government's authority.

Another approach for explaining the growth of dependency in America is the shifting paradigm of negative and positive rights. According to professor of law Antonio-Carlos Pereira-Menaut, positive rights "belong more to the tradition of increasing the power of the state to promote more safety, health, or wealth than to the constitutional tradition of limiting power."[16] Positive rights call for a more active role for the government, while negative rights call for a more limited role. The theory behind negative rights states that the less interference an individual faces from other humans, and government, the freer that individual is.[17]

America's founders emphasized negative rights over positive rights. They were afraid that a tyrannical government would oppress the people if not carefully constrained. The Bill of Rights was adopted in 1791 to appease the Anti-Federalists, espousers of negative rights who feared the expanse of the federal government and wanted many more rights to be retained by the states, as with the defunct Articles of Confederation. As George Clinton argued in *The Anti-Federalist Papers, 1778*, under the pen name Cato, if the government is not restricted from action, eventually it will act, and it may not act in the interest of the people.

Both positive and negative rights can vastly improve society, or they can destroy society. It is how they are implemented that determines the outcome. Balanced properly, positive and negative rights will set the path for prosperity. Left unbalanced, it could lead to destruction or complete oppression. Positive rights have gained greater acceptance throughout American history, in parallel with the increased activities of the government. This constant interplay between positive and negative rights plays a significant role in the analysis of the growth of dependence. And we will see that they affect the potency and prevalence of work.

The Civil War and its immediate aftermath were a turning point in American history. It was after the Civil War that individual American citizens were first guaranteed positive rights, particularly in the passage of the Civil Rights and Reconstruction Acts (1864 and 1865, respectively) as well as the amendments that soon followed. For instance, the government guaranteed and actively sought to ensure that all individuals be treated equally. The government moved away

from *protecting* individuals, to *regulating* how individuals inter-
acted with one another. The Reconstruction Amendments
exemplify this paradigm shift best. The Thirteenth,
Fourteenth, and Fifteenth Amendments all give Congress
the power to enforce the amendment through legislation.
These Amendments (which, to be clear, accomplished good
and necessary ends) stand in stark contrast to the previous
ones, which all prohibited Congress *from* acting.

The next wave of regulation came in the late 1800s and
gained force in the early twentieth century. It was led by
intellectuals, writers, and social reformers unhappy with the
effects of the industrial revolution upon the citizenry. While
it would take years before most federal regulations were implemented, one area in particular received early attention and a
quick response. After the publication of Upton Sinclair's *The
Jungle*, a horrified President Theodore Roosevelt sent investi-
gators to confirm the accuracy of the book. Once confirmed,
the Meat Inspection Act was rapidly passed by Congress. In
addition, the Food and Drug Act of 1906 was created in
response to misinformation and dangerous additives and
substitutes in both food and medicine that the American
public was ingesting daily. These items included "soothing
syrups" used for teething children, which, unbeknownst to
mothers, contained cocaine as well as narcotics.[18]

The shift of medicine and food production from the community to national companies left citizens vulnerable to poor
or even dangerously manufactured items. An erosion of trust
in the free market led to a greater acceptance of governmental
intervention. This added substantially to the drift of public
opinion toward government control and regulation.

It was no longer reasonable or physically possible for
individuals to monitor the ingredients within all consumer
items being sold to them, though, as Harvey Wiley (the
first commissioner of the Food and Drug Administration)

originally advocated in front of the Senate, he only wished for the items to be exposed for what they were, and for the consumer to make the choice themselves.[19] This again shows the contrasting views on the proper role of the government. Should the government actively monitor and ban substances, or should they simply demand labeling of products and let the consumers make the choice for themselves?

As a result of the Food and Drug Act of 1906, and other related legislation that followed, the average American consumer became dependent on the government for information. An individual can safely assume that anything they purchase in the grocery store today will not cause them serious harm in the immediate future, barring allergic reactions. If the government removed the bans, but preserved the requirement of accurate labels, today's consumers would be at a severe disadvantage, needing to do research into various chemicals and ingredients, and spending hours reading labels in the store. Americans have sacrificed choice for comfort in this situation. Most would say that this is an acceptable choice, but it still causes dependency.

Woodrow Wilson's presidency (1913–21) signaled a major change in political philosophy, and thus the role of the government. Wilson, a political scientist and former president of Princeton University, brought a new set of ideas regarding the executive branch of the government to Washington, which he had developed as a doctoral student at Johns Hopkins University. It was there that Wilson was introduced to the Hegelian concept of an "organic state" by a certain Professor George Morris.[20] The organic state inherently clashes with the idea of constitutions. Constitutions are stable texts used to interpret law and to guide the actions of the government. Under the organic state, laws are created through "organic processes," which are determined through a general sense of a fluid, changing society.[21] Under the influence of such intellectual currents, Wilson spoke of moving away from a constitutional government: "Let us break with our formulas, therefore. It will not do to look at men congregated in bodies politic through the medium of the constitutions and traditions of the states they live in, as if that were the glass of interpretation. Constitutions are vehicles of life, but not sources of it."[22] In contrast to the constitutional form of government, the organic state was more adaptable to society. Wilson believed that as time went by, old laws would simply "die" as they diverged from society's changing morality. Under these principles, it would be simple to move away from a constitutional government, even without removing the government itself. The organic state would naturally open the door to more dependency by increasing spheres of government action.

Once elected to the presidency, Wilson put these ideas into action and immediately set about reshaping the American government. In an unprecedented move, Wilson addressed Congress directly about the urgency of moving forward with his agenda. This was the first time a president had appeared during a congressional session since John Adams, and this act would become the first modern State of the Union Address.[23]

In the subsequent years of his first term, Wilson was able to pass the Underwood Tariff Act, which lowered tariffs in order to lower the cost of living for lower- and middle-class citizens; the Clayton Anti-Trust and Federal Fair Trade Commission Acts, which gave more power to labor unions and further regulated business; the Federal Reserve Act, which created the federal reserve and centralized the banking system; and the Sixteenth and Seventeenth Amendments to the Constitution, directly electing senators and authorizing the income tax. Each piece of legislation represents an expansion of the federal government, some of which did not immediately change the image of America, but all of which would in the future. The shear amount of major legislation exemplifies Wilson's annexation of power for the federal government. The amazing part of Wilson's expansion of power is that he accomplished it under no true existing crisis.[24]

But it was Franklin D. Roosevelt who transformed the character of the American government and the expectations of the American people, more than anyone before or after him. Unlike Wilson, who was a calculated intellectual more concerned with political theory and the structure within which society and the government functioned, Roosevelt was more concerned about acting today and helping the American people. President Roosevelt turned the presidency into a seat of vast power, from which he was able to influence every aspect of American life.

One of the worst crises in American history, the Great Depression, enabled Franklin Roosevelt to transform the American presidency into what it is today. He was also president for most of World War II. As warned by James Madison, "War is the mother of executive aggrandizement."[25] Cynical though it may sound, these conditions were perfect for an active executive, one who moved quickly to solve problems. At his inaugural speech, Roosevelt said, "This Nation asks for action, and action now."[26] Roosevelt believed that he was in tune with the national interest and his actions were supported by the people.

Roosevelt called on Congress and passed the Emergency Banking Act within a week of being in office.[27] Additionally, he created the Agricultural Adjustment Administration, the National Recovery Administration, and the Tennessee Valley Authority. The first hundred days of Roosevelt's presidency were "the most concentrated period of legislative activity in American history; it was also the most intense period of presidential influence in the legislative process."

One of Roosevelt's greatest—and most controversial—governmental expansions was Social Security. In essence, Social Security was created as a pension system for all American workers. According to a 1934 Brookings Institution report cited by Robert Wagner, the Senate sponsor of the Social Security Act, almost half of American families could afford to save only 1 percent or less of their incomes. The inability to save forced the elderly to continue working or to become dependent on the younger generations. In creating a national pension system, younger generations were relieved of the burden of their elderly family members (although they would still pay for them indirectly through payroll taxes). Additionally, it would free up jobs for younger generations by incentivizing the elderly to retire and collect their Social Security Benefits.[28] Ideally, this would lead to lower unemployment. Under this law, every single American citizen who earns money during his or her lifetime is directly impacted by the federal government. There is no opting out of Social Security, as it is a compulsory statutory social investment. This law is one of the major turning points in conveying a sense of government dependency and social entitlement to the American people.

It was during World War II that Roosevelt set even more important precedents. "Congress delegated sweeping powers to the President; the consequence was an enduring erosion of legislative authority."[29] Roosevelt expanded his powers in a multitude of ways, from executive orders, like the one concerning Japanese internment camps, to being involved in the war to an unprecedented degree.

During the war, President Franklin D. Roosevelt addressed what he saw as inadequacies in the founding of the country. So grave were these weaknesses that he created his own "Economic Bill of Rights." The original Bill of Rights is focused on protecting individuals from the government.

Roosevelt's new economic rights imply government assistance in practically every area of one's life. Under these rights, if a family lacked a "decent home," the government would have to guarantee that family a decent home or else provide one. These economic rights were used by Roosevelt to support his New Deal programs, and many laws today are aimed at fulfilling these goals. For example, the US Department of Housing and Urban Development facilitates in giving mortgages to subprime borrowers, or borrowers who under normal conditions would not be able to qualify for a loan.

One of the outgrowths of the Great Depression and World War II was the idea that government spending stimulates the economy, a theory promulgated by the British economist John Maynard Keynes. Keynes believed that the government should play a larger role and act as a "steering wheel" for the economy.[30] The government should adjust spending and tax rates in order to stimulate the economy (or put the brakes on such spending when the economy appeared to be getting overheated, risking inflation). Such an idea cuts against the principles of limited government upon which the constitution is based. So how was Keynesianism accepted into the mainstream? The short answer is the Great Depression. Nobody wanted to feel the pain of such an economic collapse again. The government's spending during World War II appeared to have helped pull America out of the Depression. And while Roosevelt was perhaps not a full-blown Keynesian, at important moments he did act like one.

Additionally, the years after the Depression were prosperous. So much so that a conservative and former monetarist (an opposing economic viewpoint), President Richard M. Nixon, famously said, "We are all Keynesians now." The growth in the early 1960s was off the charts. In 1965, Gross National Product grew by $14 billion, or 5 percent. In 1965 the *New York Times* summed up the boom: "Among the other new records: auto production rose 22%, steel production 6%, capital spending 16%, personal income 7% and corporate profits 21%."[31] This was generally explained by lower tax policies put in place by JFK and increases in public spending.

It is unnecessary to debate here the validity or effectiveness of the Keynesian economic model. For my purposes we need only recognize that it was an idea that changed the course of American government and thus dependency. Keynesian economics would be used as a reason to expand government and as additional support for those arguing for new expensive federal programs. Needless to say, as government spending increases, its power and its impact increase as well.

Once the Depression ended, what little safety net was in place remained predominantly reliant on individual's own efforts and help from others. Benefits were small and limited to those who deserved them. If an American received Social Security or Workers' Compensation, both New Deal programs, it was because they were not able to or were not expected to be able to take care of themselves. Aid to Families with Dependent Children (AFDC) was intended for widows with children, and Unemployment Insurance was a temporary safety net for those who lost their jobs through no fault of their own. These programs were intended for people who were unlucky and in a time of *temporary* need. The New Deal programs were not intended to help people just because they were poor or were born into a crummy situation. In the late 1950s, problems started to develop with AFDC. It was being used for a group it was never intended to support: never-married mothers with multiple children. As the number of families on AFDC increased dramatically, bolstered by growth in this new category, family size increased as well, from an average of 3.28 children in 1940 to a high of 3.89 in 1970.[32] The program made livable a lifestyle that was otherwise financially unsustainable.

In 1962, in response to the emerging facts about AFDC and the backlash against subsidizing "illegitimate" children, President John F. Kennedy proposed a new approach. Kennedy proposed a focus on assisting those in need not with money, but with social services and training. Theoretically, this would enable Americans to help themselves out of poverty. This theory would remain in place through 1964. But from 1964 to 67 with the launching of President Lyndon Johnson's Great Society there was a significant increase in income transfer benefits, contrary to JFK's proposal.

From the 1950s through the early 1970s, the United States experienced unprecedented increases in income and wealth. Median family income rose from $32,393 in 1953 to $56,475 in 1973 (in constant 2013 dollars).[33] And in these same years, spending on federal benefits for individuals soared by more than 600 percent.[34] Such dramatic figures should have produced an equally dramatic decline in the poverty rate. The number of Americans living in poverty was already in rapid decline before the 1960s. Yet as spending reached higher and higher levels, the number below poverty leveled off, even as typical family incomes rose.

President Lyndon Johnson and his Great Society program of the mid-1960s were primarily responsible for the explosion in the cost of federal poverty programs. The Great Society implemented legislation, such as Food Stamps, Medicaid, Medicare, housing subsidies, and expanded aid for education. Most of these legislative accomplishments represented new arenas of government action, others, expansions of old ones. This would be the first time that the federal government was providing individuals with a targeted means to obtain food, the first time they would be aiding individuals (other than veterans) with health-care coverage.[35]

Medicare and Medicaid were implemented in order to insure the poor who could not afford private coverage.

Medicare was targeted for seniors, while Medicaid was targeted at the broader population in poverty. The government would also be assisting the development of new medical facilities to accommodate the billions of dollars of additional demand.[36]

Housing subsidies were seen as a triumph by some, as they enabled the poor and those who faced racial discrimination to afford housing above their natural means. Housing subsidies would ideally improve the lives of the poor by providing them with a good stable living environment. Additionally, they would help reduce residential segregation (which happened without the persuasion of law).[37]

The expansion of aid for education was especially important under the Great Society, because it supported the premise that raising human capital was the solution to ending poverty. If local schools were better funded, education would improve, and thus poverty would diminish.[38]

But the culture of dependency goes beyond the programs themselves—something even deeper has changed to de-stigmatize the use of these programs.

In 1966, Richard Cloward and Frances Fox Piven published their revolutionary article in *The Nation*, "The Weight of the Poor: A Strategy to End Poverty." The plan was to overload the current welfare system in order to force the instatement of an "improved" national system. With the self-created crisis, welfare would be nationalized, as has so often happened in American history. This would eliminate the inadequacies and the stigma of collecting welfare. (How ironic that these left leaning academic activists would find themselves in bed with President Nixon who, if he had not resigned, might well have passed the national guaranteed annual income proposed by Daniel Patrick Moynihan.) Were Cloward and Piven successful? Well, they were definitely successful in raising the number of enrollees.

The emergence of welfare rights groups accompanied a rapid rise in the number of persons receiving AFDC benefits. The number of recipients increased slowly during the 1950s, but then exploded in the 1960s. The fastest growth was between 1965 and 1975, when enrollment grew by 256 percent.[39]

We see in this movement the organized beginnings of welfare entitlement, work degradation, and an eroding of the work ethic. Regrettably, much of this remains today.

Another way we have removed the stigma of welfare is by shifting the blame for poverty onto the government. America has long struggled with the causes of poverty, and the villain in the story has shifted over the years. Rooted in its tradition of personal initiative and individualism, the American people traditionally believed that poverty was a failure of character, and not the fault of society. Some call this victim blaming. Others call it personal responsibility. Over the last fifty years, however, America has seen a growing proportion of citizens believing that the poor are victims of circumstance, social injustice, or some other personally uncontrollable cause. In a 2001 survey, respondents answered the question "Which is the bigger cause of poverty today: people not doing enough or circumstances beyond their control?" with 48 percent saying "not doing enough" and a full 45 percent pointing to "circumstances."[40] For a country founded on individualism, these findings are shocking.

When the social work profession emerged a century ago, it sought to bring more attention to poverty while still upholding social values such as the work ethic. In the 1960s, however, the profession adopted advocacy for the poor and tended to blame all their problems on the society.[41]

This shift in attitude likely has a lot to do with the organization of local welfare rights activists. As they promoted the idea that welfare was a right, they changed our conception of poverty as a personal fault, with its attendant shameful feelings, to one of deserved entitlement with a full removal of blame. The causes of poverty in America do vary, but they are not across the board solely the fault of all poor individuals or solely the fault of societal circumstances. But welfare assistance is not a right, except perhaps for those unable to support themselves, and it should not be portrayed as such. Spreading the image that the poor are all victims of circumstance only further engrains the idea that they should not bother trying to remedy their situation because it is out of their control and they are anyway deserving of government assistance.

## Today

> *"The health of a democratic society may be measured by the quality of functions performed by private citizens."*
> —Alexis de Tocqueville, *Democracy in America*

Since FDR, the expansion of welfare and welfare-related programs as well as Social Security has been astonishing. We now spend on these some $360 billion a year. And to what end? Poverty remains no matter how much cash we throw at wasteful programs. Inequality continues regardless of the increased income transfers and in-kind assistance. We have become a nation that appears to prefer dependency over work. But unlike the assumption by Governor Romney that 47 percent of our country wants to be dependent (a figure he arrived at by including Social Security, a calculation with which I disagree), it is more the policies of our government that encourage it. What we need is a return to work. And that can be accomplished by the elimination of welfare and poverty programs, freeing up their funds to support job creation for those previously dependent.

Fewer and fewer American citizens are producing, while more are depending on government assistance. Through tax deductions and subsidized products, the government's reach has expanded out of control. According to Michael Grunwald, a columnist at *Time* magazine, his whole life is subsidized. From subsidies for his energy-efficient windows, flood insurance, and television to tax deductions for his mortgage, children, and home office expenses, there is little that he pays full price for.[42] If de Tocqueville is right, then America's democracy is suffering from a grave illness. According to the *Washington Examiner* columnist Timothy Carney, "The safety net is supposed to keep you from hitting rock bottom. As entitlements and handouts are expanded to the middle class and above, the net becomes more of a web, ensnaring those who would otherwise be self-sufficient."[43] The government is robbing individuals of the ability to function on their own. The safety net is no longer to assist those in need; it has steadily expanded to "ensnare" a near majority.

Some government programs function like Social Security, a mandatory quasi-retirement fund for all Americans; almost no working individual is excluded from this program (except some local and state government employees). Many other federal programs, however, were developed to assist a target group, generally the poor, or those who could not afford the necessities of life, for example, medical coverage. But in practice they have expanded far beyond their original mandate. Medicare was first enacted because some seniors had trouble paying their medical bills, but because the program covers all elderly, even the affluent, it has become hugely expensive. Medicare spent $518 billion in 2014, second only to Social Security.[44] Medicare recently expanded even further to cover prescription drugs, which it did not originally. Today, Medicare has nearly monopolized health insurance for the elderly.[45] Thus the safety net has expanded over time.

One of President Obama's signature initiatives was passing the Patient Protection and Affordable Care Act of 2010, otherwise known as Obamacare. Whatever his noble goals were, you cannot deny that it meant an expansion of government power and intervention in even more areas. Obamacare is intended to protect individuals already insured; increase choice in insurance plans, especially for those who have been rejected; attempt to decrease the cost of insurance; strengthen Medicare; make it easier for businesses to insure employees; and encourage participation in the insurance market by penalizing those who do not buy insurance. According to proponents of the new health-care law, more civilians are being protected from the evils of the "market economy." Health care is seen as a right, and because there is a difficulty in obtaining it, the government sees itself as the arbiter of justice, supplying the citizenry with an opportunity to obtain insurance.

During the Republican primary election of 2012, Newt Gingrich insulted President Obama by claiming he was the "Food Stamp President," having put more people on Food Stamps than ever before.[46] Indeed, the food stamp rolls have increased by over 19 million, or by more than two-thirds, since Obama was elected. While the president cannot be held responsible for this entire increase, as historically recipients do increase during recessions, the rolls have continued to grow even since the recession ended. In 2013, a record 47.6 million Americans (or 15 percent of the population) received this benefit, costing nearly $80 billion annually.[47]

What does this state of affairs suggest? First, that government should make efforts to grow no larger and to minimize its footprint. With respect to my prescriptions in this book, government must direct but leave delivery to nongovernmental entities. Or as Professor Steve Savas, an expert on privatization, states: "Government should steer, not row." We must as a nation return to what has worked—and that is work itself. The Protestant work ethic spurred remarkable and unprecedented growth and personal income.[48] Financial support from the government has not, and perhaps has had the opposite impact. We need jobs not welfare. If we execute my proposed policy it will finally eliminate most poverty in the United States, create jobs, and substitute work for welfare. And it will cost less than what we now spend to keep people idle.

## Notes

1. James Dorn, *Cato's Letter #12: The Rise of Government and the Decline of Morality* (Washington, DC: Cato Institute, 1996).

2. David B. Muhlhausen and Patrick Tyrrell, *The 2013 Index of Dependence on Government* (Washington, DC: Heritage Foundation, November 21, 2013); Robert Rector, *The War on Poverty: 50 Years of Failure* (Washington, DC: Heritage Foundation, September 23, 2014); *Welfare Indicators and Risk Factors: Thirteenth Report to Congress* (Washington, DC: U.S. Department of Health and Human Services, 2014); Office of Management and Budget, *Budget of the United States Government Fiscal 2015: Historical Tables* (Washington, DC: Office of Management and Budget, 2014), table 6.1.

3. For examples of these arguments, see the following: https://thedinnertableblog.wordpress.com/2011/12/15/exploding-the-myth-that-the-poor-got-poorer/ and http://www.heritage.org/research/reports/2011/09/understanding-poverty-in-the-united-states-surprising-facts-about-americas-poor.

4. http://www.heritage.org/research/reports/2012/02/2012-index-of-dependence-on-government.

5. Sara Murray, "Nearly Half of U.S. Lives in Household Receiving Government Benefit," *Wall Street Journal*, October 5, 2011.

6. http://aspe.hhs.gov/hsp/indicators02/appa-tanf.htm.

7. Michael Tanner, *The American Welfare State: How We Spend Nearly $1 Trillion a Year Fighting Poverty—and Fail* (Washington, DC: Cato Institute, April 11, 2012), 4–8.

8.  U.S. Social Security Administration, *Annual Statistical Supplement, 2013* (Washington, DC: U.S. Social Security Administration, February 14, 2014), table 5.A17.

9.  http://www.heritage.org/research/reports/2014/09/the-war-on-poverty-after-50-years.

10. Muhlhausen and Tyrrell, "2013 Index of Dependence," chart 1. http://www.heritage.org/research/reports/2013/11/the-2013-index-of-dependence-on-government.

11. Tanner, "American Welfare State," 4–6.

12. Abraham Mosisa, "Trends in Labor Force Participation in the United States," *Monthly Labor Review* 129, no. 10 (2006): 35–57. Bls. gov. Bureau of Labor Statistics, October 2006. Web. January 19, 2015; see also https://research.stlouisfed.org/fred2/series/CIVPART

13. "Databases, Tables & Calculators by Subject," Bureau of Labor Statistics Data. Bureau of Labor Statistics, January 17, 2015. Web. January 17, 2015.

14. Gary D. Alexander, 'Welfare's Failure *and the Solution*," presentation at the American Enterprise Institute, Washington, DC, July 2012.

15. Quoted in Gerald F. Seib, "In Crisis, Opportunity for Obama," *Wall Street Journal*, November 21, 2008.

16. Antonio C. Pereira-Menaut, "Against Positive Rights," *Valparaiso University Law Review* 22, no. 2 (1988): 359–83.

17. Isaiah Berlin, "Two Concepts of Liberty," in *Democracy: A Reader*. eds. Ricardo Blaug and John Schwarzmantel (New York: Columbia University Press, 2001), 155–65.

18. Donna J. Wood, "The Strategic Use of Public Policy: Business Support for the 1906 Food and Drug Act," *Business History Review* 59, no. 3 (Autumn 1985): 403–32.

19. Wood, "Strategic Use of Public Policy."

20. Christian Rosser, "Woodrow Wilson's Administrative Thought and German Political Theory," *Public Administration Review* 70, no. 4 (July/August 2010): 547–56.

21. Woodrow Wilson, "The Law and the Facts: Presidential Address, Seventh Annual Meeting of the American Political Science Association," *American Political Science Review* 5, no. 1 (February 1911): 1–11.

22.  Ibid., 10.
23.  Robert Dallek, "Woodrow Wilson, Politician," *Wilson Quarterly* 15, no. 4 (Autumn 1991): 106-14.; Edward S.Corwin, "Woodrow Wilson and the Presidency," *Virginia Law Review* 42, no. 6 (1956): 761-83.
24.  Dallek, "Woodrow Wilson."
25.  Thomas E. Cronin and William R. Hochman. "Franklin D. Roosevelt and the American Presidency," *Presidential Studies Quarterly* 15, no. 2 (Spring 1985): 277-86.
26.  Cronin and Hochman, "Franklin D. Roosevelt and the American Presidency."
27.  Ibid.
28.  Robert F. Wagner, "Is the Administration's Program for Old-Age Pensions Sound?," *Congressional Digest* 14, no. 3 (March 1935): 80-82.
29.  See note 72 above.
30.  Hyman P. Minsky, "The Legacy of Keynes," *Journal of Economic Education* 16, no. 1 (Winter 1985): 5-15.
31.  "We Are All Keynesians Now," *Time Magazine*, December 31, 1965, p. 74.
32.  http://www.gpo.gov/fdsys/pkg/GPO-CPRT-105WPRT37945/pdf/GPO-CPRT-105WPRT37945-2-7.pdf, p. 402.
33.  U.S. Bureau of the Census, *Historical Income Tables*, table F-1.
34.  Office of Management and Budget, *Budget of the United States Government, 2015: Historical Tables*, table 6.1.
35.  Adam Yarmolinsky, "The 'Great Society' - Another American Dream?," *The World Today* 24, no. 5 (May 1968): 203-8. Sar A. Levitan and Robert Taggart, "The Great Society Did Succeed," *Political Science Quarterly* 91, no. 4 (Winter 1976-1977): 601-18.
36.  John R. Stark, "The Economic Case for the Great Society," *Challenge* 15, no. 3 (January/February 1967): 22-25.
37.  Levitan and Taggart, "The Great Society Did Succeed."
38.  Stark, "Economic Case for the Great Society."
39.  U.S. Administration for Children and Families, *Temporary Assistance for Needy Families Program*, appendix table 2.1.
40.  Lisa F. Parmelee, "Among Us Always," *Public Perspective* (2002): 17-24. March 2002. Web. January 19, 2015.

41. Walter I. Trattner, *From Poor Law to Welfare State: A History of Social Welfare in America*, 3rd ed. (New York: Free Press, 1984), chaps. 11–12, 15.

42. Michael Grunwald,. "One Nation on Welfare. Living Your Life on the Dole," *Time*, September 17, 2012.

43. Timothy Carney, "Romney Gets it All Wrong on Government Dependency." *Washington Examiner*, September 12, 2012.

44. U.S. Congress, House, Committee on Ways and Means, *2014 Green Book: Background Material, and Data on the Programs Within the Jurisdiction of the Committee on Ways and Means* (Washington, DC: U.S. Government Printing Office, 2014), introduction to Medicare.

45. Jim DeMint. *Now or Never: Saving America from Economic Collapse* (New York: Center Street, 2012).

46. "Newt and the 'Food-stamp President'," *The Economist*, January 18, 2012.

47. Supplemental Nutrition Assistance Program Participation and Costs, from web page of the U.S. Department of Agriculture, http://www.fns.usda.gov/pd/supplemental-nutrition-assistance-program-snap. U.S. population figure from U.S. Department of Commerce, Bureau of the Census, *Income and Poverty in the United States: 2013*, Series P-60, No. 249 (Washington, DC: U.S. Government Printing Office, September 2014), table B-1.

48. Samuel P. Huntington, *Who Are We? The Challenges to America's National Identity* (New York: Simon & Schuster, 2004), chap. 4.

# 3

# Why Have We Become
# a Nation of Takers?

> *"Washington is building a culture of depen-*
> *dency, with ever-more people relying on an*
> *ever-growing federal government to give*
> *them cash or benefits."*
> —Mathew Spaulding[1]

Despite all of the well-meaning spending that has been devoted to poverty over the past decades, the American people have seen little to no improvement for their money. Between 1964 and 2014 federal and state governments spent $19 trillion on antipoverty programs.[2] The poverty rate, already in rapid decline before the War on Poverty programs were even implemented, was at just over 15 percent in 1964. It would drop to a low of 11.1 percent by 1973, but today is back up to 14.5 percent.[3] The goal of the War on Poverty was to eradicate poverty forever—yet over $19 trillion has been spent for a net change of 4.5 percentage points, and the programs' lasting positive effects have been so fragile that we may soon be back where we started. For those in extreme poverty, the results are even worse. Between the same years, the percentage of the population subsisting at 50 percent of the poverty level or below has decreased less than 1 percentage point from 6.2 percent to 5.4 percent. Compassion and benevolence are likely driving these programs, because they clearly are not justified based on results.

The government has focused mostly on alleviating pains, rather than changing individuals' underlying situations, treating the symptoms but not the disease. Very few anti-poverty programs focus on lifting individuals out of poverty, rather than making them more comfortable in poverty. The welfare reform of 1996 (Personal Responsibility and Work Opportunity Reconciliation Act) is one example of forcing the poor to help themselves, but this is only one of the 126 programs run by the federal government today. Additionally, some of the programs that are aimed toward helping those in poverty to help themselves have had meager results, notably Head Start and federal training programs, which have shown only minimal gains in skills or earnings.[4] The government's insistence on tinkering with people's lives has led to stagnation in poverty, a bloated budget, and bureaucracy with few results.

Yet, crucially, even as poverty rates have fluctuated, dependency has steadily increased. This makes sense. The government was increasing direct cash transfers (increases in welfare benefits) and in-kind contributions (like public housing). These had the effect of moderating the effects of poverty by the expansion of income. But the irony is that as we focused on reducing poverty, we increased reliance on the state for our monetary and personal needs.

At the same time, those of us newly engaged in the War on Poverty also promulgated the idea of victimization as a justification for government action: the poor's woeful condition was a direct result of what society and others had done *to* them and so payback was required. Poverty was therefore not a result of any personal failings. It was a by-product of purposeful actions on the part of some members of society to beat down the poor and keep them enslaved. It never occurred to us then that we were sowing the seeds of a cancer that would help fire up the victimization movements of the late 1960s and beyond.

Perhaps at the heart of the compassion for the poor shown by the liberals was, as Charles Sykes says in his book, A *Nation of Moochers*, an assumption of incompetence. In this view, the poor are victims who must be protected, and thus government must do for them what they cannot do for themselves. The government then increasingly becomes responsible for running your life. However, there is extreme danger here to individual liberty. As Friedrich Hayek wrote, dependence can lead to serfdom.

Let's examine a few of the programs that were started in the mid-1960s and evaluate their ultimate effectiveness. Most of these programs assumed widespread incompetence among the poor, requiring government to right the wrongs of the society that produced the conditions for poverty. This is not an exhaustive review, but merely a recounting of some of the most telling examples of how and why programs failed, yet continued to receive support.

## Head Start

Who could argue with the call for early childhood education for the poor? Studies galore suggested that children from low-income families were less prepared for entrance to school and thus lagged behind others throughout high school. In one study, researchers found that after the first four years of life, higher-income children were exposed to as many as 30 million more words than children of low-income families, with lasting impacts on language and educational performance later in life.[5] Clearly, getting to these children early and delivering the education that other more prosperous children were receiving in their homes could only be positive. But this is not what happened.

Head Start claims that it "promotes the school readiness of children ages birth to 5 from low-income families by enhancing their cognitive, social and emotional development." But the government's own evaluations have shown that it does not succeed in doing this. The Department of Health and Human Services (HHS) released its latest findings of a long study that followed Head Start kids all the way to third grade. They found that "by third grade, the $8 billion Head Start program had little to no impact on cognitive, social-emotional, health, or parenting practices of participants. On a few measures, access to Head Start had harmful effects on children."[6]

In *Launching the War on Poverty*, Michael Gillette quotes D. Baker, a planner in that war (who uses the conventional racial language of the time): "Perhaps in some respects the worst thing about [Head Start] was that in many areas it was converted from a child-oriented program to a public employment program for adult Negroes. They were hiring illiterate, untrained Negroes and not infrequently requiring a certain amount of militancy from them [to] in essence baby sit the children—at least that was our evaluation, in order to spread the loot."[7]

Joe Klein, one of our nation's leading journalists, categorically declares Head Start a monumental failure. "It is now 45 years since this program was begun. Today, we spend more than $7 billion each year on the Head Start program, serving over 1 million children." Klein continues, writing that "there is indisputable evidence about the program's effectiveness, provided by the Department of Health and Human Services: Head Start does not work. . . . Head Start graduates performed about the same as students of similar income and social status who were not part of the program." Klein reports that "these results were so shocking that the HHS team sat on them for several years." Correctly, he observes that Head Start is representative of many government-run social programs. They often succeed as pilot programs but fail when taken to full scale.

One simple question reveals why Head Start was doomed from the start: why is Head Start administered through HHS and not the Department of Education? The answer—it was part of LBJ's War on Poverty directive. His vision was to have community action programs (i.e., local agencies) administer programs to rebuild poor communities. Head Start was to be a signature community action program. In Klein's telling, "these outfits soon proved slovenly; often they were little more than patronage troughs for local Democratic Party honchos—and, remarkably, to this day, they remain the primary dispensers of Head Start funds." These community action agencies that administer Head Start today are really facilitating "make work" jobs. Ironically, Head Start became a jobs program, rather than an early education program!

But there are much better ways to educate children and to find people jobs than Head Start. As Klein concludes, since we are talking about the lives of children, "This is criminal. Head Start is in one sense a metaphor for federal government waste and inefficiency—a noble idea that does not work. Instead, it has become a government patronage machine that swallows up $7 billion annually and does not really aid the children it is supposed to help. So, it is actually a case study for the waste and lack of integrity of the national government."[8]

This is not a condemnation of early childhood programs. Instead, it is a scathing indictment of the way this specific social welfare program was mounted. Again, the parallel institutions of municipal government and advocacy groups undermined whatever accomplishments might have been achieved from a good idea. Local community groups should not have been brought on board to do this work. It should have been the purview of the Department of Education with oversight by the local electorate through their existing school boards. But it was not. Worst of all, politicians refuse to acknowledge the disaster for fear of offending interest groups. And so Head Start continues to suck up money without producing results.

When I wrote to Klein, asking if there was any hope for changing Head Start, he replied, "Obama has started a Race to the Top program for Head Start—he's closing down some of the worst ones, starting new ones mostly through local school systems. It's way too soon to tell if it's working, though." Closing down the worst Head Start programs is a step in the right direction, but even shifting responsibility to local school systems is no panacea. My fear is that since most Head Start is targeted to minority poor children who reside in school districts with the poorest performance, this just won't fix the problem. The mayor of New York has recently proposed universal early childhood education. Although he wanted to tax the rich for this (he was stymied by Governor Cuomo on this part) this move by Mayor de Blasio might go a long way in replacing ineffective Head Start programs.

## Job Corps

Job Corps was another major weapon in the War on Poverty. For LBJ, this program was personal—based on his experience operating youth programs in Texas, he was convinced that training and education, delivered in a residential setting, would impart the human capital required for obtaining jobs and moving out of poverty. The Civilian Conservation Corps (CCC) had employed young men to work in rural areas helping with conservation projects. It trained and educated them and was widely seen as a valuable way to alleviate unemployment caused by the depression. Between

1933 and 1942, more than 3 million men were employed by the CCC.[9] These weren't long-term jobs by any means, and the numbers certainly fell short of FDR's predictions that the CCC would employ a million men per year (the maximum was three hundred thousand in any given year). Yet even though the CCC didn't have a lasting effect on unemployment, it was successful in that it contributed to infrastructure projects, provided some short-term economic stimulus, and gave short-term jobs to a limited number of young men who were unemployed yet eager to work. Based on LBJ's positive experience with the CCC, Job Corps centers have been established in 125 locations and have served more than 2 million youth since its inception. However, as with so many of well-intentioned programs, we see results that have fallen far short of the mission's goals.[10]

The Heritage Foundation has reported that the federal government spends about $1.5 billion per year on Job Corps,[11] and scientific evaluations have demonstrated that the federal government gets little in return on its investment. A recent impact evaluation of Job Corps ("2008 outcome study"), published in the December 2008 issue of the *American Economic Review*, employed a randomized experiment—the "gold standard" of scientific research—to assess the impact of Job Corps on participants compared to similar individuals who did not participate in the program.

For a federal taxpayer investment of $25,000 per Job Corps participant, the 2008 outcome study found the following[12]:

- Compared to nonparticipants, Job Corp participants were less likely to earn a high school diploma (7.5 percent vs. 5.3 percent).
- Compared to nonparticipants, Job Corp participants were no more likely to attend or complete college.
- Employed Job Corps participants earned $0.22 more in hourly wages compared to employed control group members.
- Four years after participating in the evaluation, the average weekly earnings of Job Corps participants was $22 more than the average weekly earnings of the control group.

Since the practice of research on public programs was only just beginning, there is little data on the CCC and its accomplishments. But we do know that because the army ran it, the professionalism was unusually high for its operations and likely much higher than what we have seen reported in evaluations of Job Corps, which remains one of the nation's most expensive education and training programs with only mixed results.[13] The American populace clearly thought it was beneficial—it was among the most popular of the new Deal programs. And the results were easily visible in the parks and on the road around them. Much of the CCC's work still stands today, in the parks, trails, and waterways that mark the American landscape.[14]

Why, then, did the Job Corps fail when by most accounts the CCC was so successful? Two reasons stand out. First, the CCC provided real jobs while the Job Corps provides only classroom training. We have seen over again at America Works that training and education has little impact on a formerly dependent or long-term-unemployed person. Studies by MDRC and others prove that getting someone a job first is the way to go.[15] Job Corps instead fell into the easy trap of choosing "bums on seats" instead of providing real jobs where the participants could learn real marketable soft and hard skills.

The second main reason was a lack of discipline. The CCC recruited mainly people affected by the Depression. The program targeted unemployed young men, veterans, and American Indians hard hit by the Great Depression. These were in large part working people who had been unexpectedly struck by the weight of unemployment. The CCC boys, as they were called, were required to send a portion of their wages home to their parents. The boys also received free education, health care, and job training.

In contrast, the Job Corps attracts principally poorly educated black youth from our inner cities. When it allows women, they generally have similar backgrounds. Plagued by a lack of clear goals, coupled with a voracious private sector ready and willing to fudge the numbers for placements into jobs or recidivism to crime, corruption has been rampant.[16]

Perhaps the Job Corps' central failing was that it was delegated to incompetent program operators paid not for results, but solely for running the programs—regardless of success. To successfully revamp this, as we have said, government should direct and hold accountable the organizations that run such efforts. If paid for their real performance—specifically, on the basis of whether participants got jobs and if they stayed in them—the Job Corps might well succeed.

## Neighborhood Youth Corps

The Neighborhood Youth Corps provides work and training for young men and women, ages sixteen to twenty-one, from impoverished families and neighborhoods. Supported in part by the Ford Foundation, local poverty programs in New Haven and on the Lower East Side of New York ran employment programs for youth. Besides work-related assistance, these neighborhood efforts included help with education, health, day care, and housing assistance. According to several General Accounting Office (GAO) reports, the program had no effect on dropout rates and did not slow increasing youth crime rates. In fact, the GAO concluded in 1969 that some youth actually "regressed in their conception of what should reasonably be required in return for wages paid."[17]

Ten years later, conditions were no better. GAO found that "almost three of every four [urban] enrollees were exposed to a worksite where good work habits were not learned or reinforced, or realistic ideas on expectations in the real world of work were not fostered."[18]

When a federal program fails, politicians can always change its name to create the appearance of reform. In 1972, after years of embarrassing failures, the name of the Neighborhood

Youth Corps was changed to the Summer Program for Economically Disadvantaged Youth. In 1977, after more exposés and boondoggles, the name was changed again to the Summer Youth Employment Program (SYEP). But the new names have masked old problems.

The NYC program and its copycat successors failed for the classic reason: training by incompetent operators for jobs that no longer exist. Instead of providing incentives for the private sector to train disadvantaged people for real jobs, the government ran outdated programs with little chance of employment at the end. Again, as with Job Corps, the way to change the program for the better is to pay for results, clearly define the goals, and let the private sector be participants in operating it. These are the only ways to give this problematic program a chance of making a difference.

## Workforce Training Efforts

Since the Great Depression ended, America has had a series of failed workforce training initiatives, all of which had little or no positive impact, some even negative. When it was created VISTA superbly fit the purposes of the War on Poverty. It was established by the Economic Opportunity Act in 1964 to recruit, select, train, and refer volunteers to state or local agencies or private nonprofit organizations to spend a year helping to deliver local poverty programs. It also encouraged local private businesses to join the effort. But what seemed like a responsible way to help reduce poverty was in fact throwing inexperienced young people at just the sort of programs we have found to be ineffective.

AmeriCorps was created in 1993 to place adult Americans in community service with nonprofit and public agencies, especially in environmental protection, health, education, and public safety. This was a second generation of VISTA. Since little exists in the way of solid evaluations of VISTA, the experience of AmeriCorps is perhaps illustrative.

In an op-ed in the *Wall Street Journal*, "The Reality of Feel-Good Government," commentator James Bovard wrote that AmeriCorps' internally generated data were hardly reflective of reality. The stated goals of the program were not measured and the GAO found that the self-reported data from grant recipients were unverified and unreliable.

Can't we now begin to see a pattern? Good intentions are converted into programs bent on benevolence, but which swell and expand despite their meager results. Vested interests develop with ties to politicians who are reluctant to retract or replace the bad with effective alternatives. Program recipients and organizers alike deliver votes. The public is either unaware or uninterested and relies on the government to do the right thing. Programs grow until they are bloated. The providers flourish. And poverty and dependence continue. There is no shaft of light focused on the process—the only shaft in view is the one given to the poor.

## Notes

1. http://www.cnn.com/2012/09/21/opinion/spalding-welfare-state-dependency/.
2. Tanner, "American Welfare State," 2.
3. Bureau of the Census, *Income and Poverty in the United States: 2013*, table B-1.
4. U.S. Administration for Children and Families, *Head Start Impact Study*; Howard S. Bloom, Larry L. Orr, Stephen H. Bell, George Cave, Fred Doolittle, Winston Lin, Johannes M. Bos, "The Benefits and Costs of JTPA Title II-A Programs: Key Findings from the National Job Training Partnership Act Study," *Journal of Human Resources* 32, no. 3 (Summer, 1997): 549–76.
5. Betty Hart and Todd R. Risley, "The Early Catastrophe: The 30 Million Word Gap by Age 3," *American Educator* Spring (2003): 4-9.
6. Michael Puma, *Head Start Research: Third Grade Follow-up to the Head Start Impact Study*, OPRE, 2012, http://www.acf.hhs.gov/sites/default/files/opre/head_start_executive_summary.pdf.
7. Gillette, *Launching the War on Poverty*, 322.

8.    Jim Eckman, "The Failure of Head Start," Issues in Perspective with Dr. Jim Eckman, July 2011, http://graceuniversity.edu/iip/2011/07/11-07-30-2/.

9.    Melissa Bass, *The Politics and Civics of National Service: Lessons from the Civilian Conservation Corps, VISTA, and Americorps* (Washington, DC: Brookings), 1.

10.   Summary of Job Corps: http://www.allgov.com/departments/department-of-labor/job-corps?agencyid=7169.

11.   David B. Muhlhausen, *Job Corps: An Unfailing Record of Failure*, The Heritage Foundation, May 2009, http://www.heritage.org/research/reports/2009/05/job-corps-an-unfailing-record-of-failure.

12.   Peter Z. Schochet, John Burghardt, and Sheena McConnell, "Does Job Corps Work? Impact Findings from the National Job Corps Study," *American Economic Review* 98, no. 5 (2008): 1864-86.

13.   http://www.gpo.gov/fdsys/pkg/GAOREPORTS-HEHS-95-180/html/GAOREPORTS-HEHS-95-180.htm; http://www.heritage.org/research/reports/2007/02/job-corps-a-consistent-record-of-failure.

14.   http://www.pbs.org/wgbh/americanexperience/features/introduction/ccc-introduction/.

15.   http://www.mdrc.org/sites/default/files/full_391.pdf, p. 28.

16.   http://www.cbsnews.com/news/federal-government-job-corps-program-investigation-raises-questions-about-effectiveness/.

17.   (GAO, *Review of Economic Opportunity Programs* (Washington DC: U.S. Government Printing Office, 1969), 70.

18.   (GAO, "More Effective Management Is Needed to Improve the Quality of the Summer Youth Employment Program," February 20, 1979)

# 4

# The Failure of Poverty Programs

> *"Billions for equal opportunity, not one cent for equal outcome."*
> —Charles Murray[1]

> *"The evaluations of specific programs that were available during the first ten years after the launching of the [War on Poverty] confirmed the verdict: nothing worked, and, in particular, nothing that one did in education worked."*
> —Nathan Glazer[2]

Most poverty programs fail. Despite that indisputable fact, they continue to receive funding every fiscal year, often at ever-increasing levels. The Department of Health and Human Services' own evaluations of its Head Start program, a need-based educational program supplemented by an array of social services for children of pre-kindergarten age, show that the positive impact is negligible and vanishes within a year after children leave the program.[3] Along with a myriad of other well-intentioned attempts to eradicate poverty, it just does not work.

There is ample evidence that most poverty programs should be scrapped or at the very least seriously revamped. For example, I would argue that the Job Corps, a US Labor Department program that administers various education, training, and job placement services, should be completely eliminated. The small gains for its clients are not worth the high cost of $16,500 per client per year.[4] Similarly, Social Security Disability Insurance must be overhauled. SSDI recipients have increased from a little over 1 percent of the working-age population in 1966 to 5 percent in 2014, even while the general health of the population has been improving.[5] There are towns in the United States where 25 percent of the population is on disability.[6] Recently, more than thirty employees of the Long Island Rail Road, a major commuter rail provider in New York, were convicted of defrauding the disability program to the tune of $1 billion.[7] Supposedly disabled employees learned jujitsu and fought fires while collecting SSDI.[8]

But nongovernmental programs rarely did any better. By their nature, many of these organizations, new to running poverty programs, were inferior to the existing ones. Their inexperience was the most limiting factor of these parallel institutions, and they weren't actually successful in moving people toward independence in society.

They survived by gaining new funds from the established political structure; quality and accountability was traded for dollars and votes. The outcomes of the programs were never a prerequisite for support. In addition, community action, by establishing itself as a parallel political alternative to city hall, created an atmosphere of antagonism that undermined any efforts to create exemplary programs. There was no reason for city hall, for instance, to cultivate competing organizations that would have spurred each other toward developing best practices. Better let them build the foundations of poverty programs on quicksand, fail, and revert in desperation to the preeminence of city hall.

In the early days of the republic, the relationship between work and success was simple. You had to work if you wanted to eat. In the centuries since, the government has interposed itself in that equation in numerous complex and disorienting ways. The result is that many recent government programs have made working irrational and receiving benefits rational. So much of what I have seen during my five decades of fighting poverty is an increase in a perverse reliance on strategies that actively make work less desirable.

On balance, the poor make rational economic decisions. If the government makes welfare more economically desirable than work, who are we to blame—the recipient or the wasteful government? Examples of backwards incentives abound. We give more money to mothers who have more children. We ease disability requirements to allow more able-bodied people to stay at home. We loosen work requirements in an effort to make welfare programs kinder and gentler. Instead of making work pay, we pay for no work. As Milton Friedman put it, "We have a system that increasingly taxes work and subsidizes non-work." This is a system that is bound for destruction.

Such programs are run in states throughout the country, and some of them are national. The benefits received include S-CHIP (child health insurance), child care, energy subsidies, housing subsidies, food subsidies (Food Stamps), earned income tax credit, and others.[9] In Wisconsin the story is similar. According to a report by the Legislative Fiscal Bureau of Wisconsin, a single parent with one child earning the poverty level salary for a family of two can almost triple his household income through state aid and poverty programs. This hypothetical individual, earning $15,130, would be eligible for $4740 in medical assistance, $3672 in assistance with food and other necessities, $10,972 for child care, $4188 in Section 8 housing, and $4485 through tax credits. That would be a total benefit of $28,057, bringing the individual's net income to $43,187. There is a clear incentive in this scenario not to work more than the minimum, much like the example in Pennsylvania.[10]

Do these incentives actually have an impact on our economy? According to the research of Casey Mulligan, a Chicago University economist, they do. Mulligan argues that the Federal Additional Compensation, COBRA subsidies, Broad-Based Categorical Eligibility, the modernization of Unemployment Insurance eligibility, the mortgage modification, and other policies have encouraged "a few million" people from working, because the government was paying them to do exactly that, not work. He goes on to argue that the redistribution of wealth through safety net programs has an economic cost, reducing labor, consumption, capital, and market output. Mulligan's research shows that the American people do respond to the economic incentives set up by the welfare state. As rules are slackened, more Americans go on the rolls. As rules are tightened, as seen by the welfare reform (PRWORA) in 1996, welfare rolls shrink.[11]

A Cato Institute report in 2013 found that welfare paid more than the entry-level job a typical welfare recipient could expect to find. It went on to conclude that the current welfare system provides such high levels of benefits that it acts as a disincentive to work. The combination of welfare and other means-tested programs pays more than the minimum wage in thirty-five states, and in thirteen states it pays more than you would earn a $15 per hour full-time job. Shockingly, in eleven states, welfare pays more than the average pretax first-year wage for a public school teacher. In thirty-nine states it pays more than the starting wage of a secretary. And in the three most generous states, it pays more than an entry-level computer programmer. Here again, welfare trumps work.[12]

As reported earlier in this book, representatives from the US Department of Agriculture came to New York City in 2012 demanding it change current policy for Supplemental Nutrition Assistance Program ("food stamp") recipients. You see, city rules stated that if you were on Food Stamps and were able-bodied, you were required to work if a job was available. In other words, as with the welfare bill of 1996, there was an expectation of reciprocal responsibility. In fact, work requirements—albeit weak ones—were also put in place in the federal legislation for food stamp recipients. But the Obama administration, in its efforts to weaken that hugely successful bill, instructed the Department of Agriculture to ignore the work requirement provisions and force New York City to pay out the benefit regardless of whether the able-bodied recipients went to work.

But wait, there's more. New York City has recently directed programs charged with finding work for people on Food Stamps not to serve even those who volunteer for the jobs! In our case that meant refusing to help veterans, homeless, and ex-offenders gain employment. Why, you might ask, would the government act so brazenly contemptuous toward getting people working and off subsidies? The 1996 welfare bill calls for work if there is a job. But city officials would contend (remember the education and training argument) that recipients would be put in jobs that were beneath them—"hamburger-flipper jobs" is their euphemism. Despite the failures of such training programs and the success of work-first, they are determined to play out their progressive theory based on nothing but that theory, despite its failure over the last many decades. Here we have a proven strategy written into the 1996 law that is being undermined by government—well intended it may seem to some, but bone headed in light of the research that proves training is an inefficient way to reduce dependency. They are right that there is some need for a kinder, gentler

way of dealing with the welfare population. Some past programs and requirements have been counterproductive and
have actually complicated the transition into jobs for some
participants. But this is a slippery slope. At America Works
the average wage for welfare recipients placed in jobs is over
$10 per hour with many food, housing, and medical benefits
along with the earned income tax credit remaining. These
are good entry-level jobs providing entrance to work and the
chance to move up.

Now to be fair, there are many in government who get it
right. Present and past administrations in Wisconsin have
conducted welfare-to-work programs in creative ways con-
sistent with the reform of the 1990s. And there are those
who previously only saw welfare recipients as selfish takers,
like Rudy Giuliani, who have come to understand that it is
in fact more the government's policies that encourage the
dependency than individual sloth.[13]

In late 2013 Representative Paul Ryan came to visit Lee
and me at our Washington, DC, offices. He spent about three
quarters of an hour in a classroom of mostly black women
on welfare. They regaled him with stories of how their case-
workers at the welfare department had discouraged them
from going to work and encouraged having more children to
increase their benefits. Upon leaving the classroom I asked
him what he had learned. He repeated Mayor Giuliani's
sentiments when he had experienced the same conversations:
"They really want to work."

I then suggested that Mitt Romney had made a mistake with
his comments that 47 percent of the country was takers from
the government. I said the mistake was that he implied that they
all *wanted* to be dependent on the government. As a conservative, I remarked, Romney and he, Ryan, should have identified
big government as the culprit. It is in fact the incentives to be

on government support and the resistance to promote work that is the hallmark of our current welfare state. To my delight he agreed, as did Eric Cantor in a similar discussion.

But sensibility has existed across the Republican/ Democratic divide. President Clinton supported and got into law the most sweeping and revolutionary change in welfare law. Reciprocal responsibility was required of able-bodied welfare recipients get welfare but work if they can. This was a monumental shift in policy and ideology brought about by our then Democratic president. While some might see my perspective throughout this book as tilting more to the right, make no mistake: I credit President Clinton, alongside Speaker Gingrich, with an irrevocable change in our country's attitude toward government support.

This resistance to work requirements began as the new welfare came into play in the late 1990s, but its roots come from liberals' attempts to minimize the importance of work in reducing dependency. Perhaps some of the first attacks came in demanding that people not be required to take low-income, dead-end jobs. Better they remain on welfare. The liberal notion that some jobs were just not good enough for poor people permeated the criticisms from the left. In Barbara Ehrenreich's book *Nickel and Dimed*, the plight of the low-wage worker is portrayed with an almost gleeful enthusiasm, as if gloating about how bad the private sector is and how badly it exploits poor welfare recipients. It is an assault on work, categorizing it as a four-letter word. But her argument fails on two counts. First, welfare recipients who work in low-wage jobs maintain many of their benefits, significantly increasing their real incomes. Second, she is ignorant of, or consciously avoids, the psychological and spiritual benefits of work. Work socializes. It gives one a sense of purpose and dignity. It nourishes the soul. One study looked at the scientific evidence on the relationship between work and health and well-being, focusing on working-age adults and the common health problems that account for the majority of long-term incapacity and sickness absence. Unemployment was shown to increase rates of sickness, disability, and mental health problems, and to decrease life expectancy. It also results in an increased use of medication, medical services, and higher hospital admission rates. Returning to work from unemployment results in significant health improvements and increases the self-esteem of individuals. The improvements in health that result from returning to work can reverse the negative health effects of unemployment. The evidence clearly demonstrates that working is generally beneficial to people's physical and mental health and overall well-being.[14]

Yet, despite the fact that people want to work, and working is good for them, it is hard to argue with the statement that workers have become more dispensable in the present economy. No one expects to have a job for life these days. Right now, because of the impending mandate under the Affordable Care Act, companies are replacing full-time jobs with place part-time ones to avoid providing health-care insurance premiums or paying a penalty. There has been a growing trend emphasizing the fungible nature of labor, where, for example, older, experienced workers are replaced with younger, less expensive ones. As this occurs, the government inevitably jumps in to provide income that the private sector no longer can. A prime example would be the extension of unemployment benefits in the face of our current recession.

We have found that the conception that certain jobs are not good enough actively prevents job placement. Training for unrealistic positions is considered absolutely more desirable than many employment opportunities. When Lee Bowes first began working in the Oakland area in the late 1990s it was as a consultant to a prisoner reentry program run by Allen Temple, a large black church that received a grant from President

Bush's Faith-Based Initiative. There she encountered a four-month-long training program for returning prisoners, aimed at preparing participants to take on skilled apprenticeship positions in the building trades. The first problem was one of supply and demand: there were tons of laid-off, experienced construction workers in the Bay area with little or no work for them. Second, the program had trouble recruiting people to sit in the classes because the young men needed money and could not afford to sit through eight hours of training over the four months. America Works, with its work-first approach, eliminated the training program and quickly started placing people in suitable employment. Our success allowed us to continue working directly in Oakland, most recently in the "realignment area." Realignment is the court-mandated early return of prisoners, some of whom were serious offenders, to their communities in order to ease prison overcrowding. Rather than supervise them through parole, these prisoners were placed under the less costly probation system. Recently, Bowes went to Oakland and spoke to some of the probation officers who have referred several such prisoners to us for job placement. There she encountered similar problems. One man who had been in prison for almost thirty years was insulted when he was offered a job at a small auto parts store for $12 an hour. The probation officer agreed with his indignation. He has a family, she said. How can you expect him to support them on a job that pays so little? Bowes explained to her that he had no work history and a murder charge, and we have a small business-owner willing to train him and give him a chance. She said, "I have never worked for as little as $12 an hour and I do not think he should have to." Six months later the man was still unemployed and very depressed.

Not only does big government get in the way when it provides disincentives to work, it also has a profoundly negative effect on community. The more the government does for individuals, the more community is diminished. I want to quote from de Tocqueville's *Democracy in America* here since he was prescient concerning the importance of community and what would happen in its absence:

> The citizen of the United States is taught from infancy to rely upon his own exertions in order to resist the evils and the difficulties of life; he looks upon the social authority with an eye of mistrust and anxiety, and he claims its assistance only when he is unable to do without it.[15]

De Tocqueville observed how liberty and the need for social cooperation give people incentives to be virtuous. But as we have seen, the gradual transfer of the production of food and medicine away from home and community powered the increase in government control and weakened our mitigating institutions.

America needs to maintain a balance between strong communities and strong institutions. With a proper balance, they provide the foundation of a successful society. The right combination of community and society can provide America with autonomy and responsibility, with minimal costs for transactions, a reduction of moral hazard, strong individuality with high participation in group networks, and reduced rent seeking. However, when government intervenes to fill the gaps that community fails to cover, the intrusion can eat away at the fabric of the community as a whole. This erosion in turn will cause further government action. Civil society atrophies.

The story of our slide into dependency would be incomplete without accounting for the antibusiness mood that has been gathering force in recent years. In the 2012 presidential election, Governor Mitt Romney was vilified for being a successful businessman. These days, business is seen as evil, and being rich is assumed to be the result of greed instead of success. In fact, businessmen have become America's favorite bad guy. In movies ranging from *Wall Street* to *It's a Wonderful Life*, the antagonist is always the evil businessman taking advantage of the innocent. But this was not always the case in America. Our mistrust of success is a new development, and a very dangerous one. It undermines the industriousness, the exceptionalism, and the independence that Americans have learned from their past.

The notion that businessmen are evil goes against America's founding virtues that productivity and the pursuit of happiness are encouraged and cause prosperity. Instead we have burgeoning class warfare, aptly represented by the Occupy Wall Street movement that briefly took hold in 2011. While the movement never achieved a coherent message, one recurring and vocal theme was a hatred of successful businessmen; they held signs saying "Eat the Rich" or "Rich beware, your days are numbered."

When class warfare takes over a segment of the population, those who believe that they are disadvantaged believe that they deserve something from the other group. They also tend to blame the majority of their problems on the other group. This attitude fosters the idea of entitlement and makes people believe that they deserve support from the government, because the government is perceived to have been catering to another group for too long.

This is not to say that the complaints of the Occupy Wall Street protests are not legitimate. There are examples of rampant corruption throughout our government, of corporate cronyism. Certain groups do have more sway than others. But attacking the rich, having the rich share, or having them "pay their fair share" will not do anything to remedy the situation.

The stance taken by Occupy Wall Street only exacerbates friction and hatred toward successful businessmen, the very people who make America successful. Capitalism has lifted more people out of poverty around the world than any other -ism. Why is this lost on the new progressives?

Work is noble, not evil. We must cherish these principles and reject the attacks that would dilute them. Moreover, while most poverty programs fail at improving people's lives and changing their situations, my experience has demonstrated that work simply *works*. Our nation has inexorably moved from reliance on a work ethic to dependence on government to sustain us. Ours is a society that expects to be supported. It is the product of those who crafted policies that chose to see people as victims, incapable of work. Little wonder, then, that they reject work as a solution.

In her article "Intangible Dividend of Antipoverty Effort: Happiness," published in the *New York Times* on September 20, 2012, Sabrina Tavernise reported, "When thousands of poor families were given federal housing subsidies in the early 1990s to move out of impoverished neighborhoods, social scientists expected the experience of living in more prosperous communities would pay off in better jobs, higher incomes and more education. That did not happen. But more than 10 years later, the families' lives had improved in another way: They reported being much happier than a comparison group of poor families who were not offered subsidies to move."

What happened here was not a full-scale new program, but rather an experiment, called Moving to Opportunity (MTO). It tested whether prospects would improve if families moved into more affluent neighborhoods. Making use of section 8 vouchers (which otherwise help pay the rent for poor people) helped them move out of the inner city. It did make the families happier, but it certainly didn't succeed in getting them off welfare. So while the basic thesis—moving poor people into prosperous communities would change their lot in life—did not prove valid in this study, the silver lining of MTO was an uptick in happiness. The commentary on this from social scientists like William Julius Wilson was that an increase in mental health is important. "Mental health and subjective well-being are very important," said Wilson, a sociology professor at Harvard whose 1987 book *The Truly Disadvantaged* pioneered theory about concentrated poverty. "If you are not feeling well, it's going to affect everything—your employment, relations with your family." No argument there. I am not undervaluing the importance of happiness, but that doesn't change that the program failed to achieve its stated goals. A more recent study, reported on by the Brookings Institution found that moving families to better neighborhood did in fact improve a number of sociopsychological factors in those studied.[16] Even so, if happiness was the objective of the MTO evaluation, perhaps other interventions might have been more productive.

As one surveys the research on poverty and the programs meant to alleviate it, this is the common theme—either the results are doctored or the odd unintended positive effect is ballyhooed.

Here is another MDRC study, so in need of positive results, that it misses the most important point. The Center for Employment Opportunities runs a work program for ex-offenders. This program, hugely expensive in comparison with other employment programs, failed to get people working because it was a transitional "make work" program. It did not put people into real, lasting jobs and thus the ex-offenders were no more likely to be employed than the control group. The key findings were as follows:

- CEO generated a large but short-lived increase in employment; the increase was driven by CEO's transitional jobs. By the end of the first year of the study period, the program and control groups were equally likely to be employed, and their earnings were similar.[17]

- CEO did improve recidivism, with reductions in the share of clients convicted or incarcerated for a new crime, especially for those who came to the program within three months of leaving prison.[18]

But these gains were expensive. The cost of the program outwardly appears to be acceptable, at $4100 per participant. However, the cost is calculated per enrollee, and not on a pay-for-performance contract, meaning that each participants costs $4100, even those that fail to obtain real employment. Only 71 percent of the program group entered CEO's transitional jobs, and "About 44 percent of those who worked in a transitional job were placed into permanent jobs, according to CEO's records." This means that only 31 percent of the starting program group was actually placed in a permanent job. For every successful participant, just over two others failed, which raises the cost of a successful job placement to $12,300. CEO's recidivism results would have been still stronger, and less costly, if it had actually put more clients to work.[19] Yet CEO is to be commended in recognizing the role work might play in reducing recidivism.

## The Role of Philanthropy

In studying what can work, foundations have continued to hold a great deal of sway over policy in the decades since their heyday in the 1960s (discussed in Chapter 1), but they have mostly left out a key partner with critical input: the private sector. One of the most pervasive qualities that have characterized these foundations has been a strong antibusiness bias. There was hardly any thought to engaging the private sector significantly in the solving of poverty. And when the private sector absolutely had to be involved, profits were anathema.

The most significant private solution was the Manpower Development Research Corp (MDRC), initiated by the Ford

Foundation. It was one of a few "intermediaries" established to broker public and foundation funds for urban programs and to evaluate them. Public Private Ventures was another (it recently went out of business). MDRC's goal was to stabilize poor neighborhoods and keep them stable for the poor who lived there. This was essentially the mantra of the War on Poverty.

MDRC organized federal housing tax credits along with foundation funding to create significant resources targeting ghetto communities. The goal was to create affordable housing and generate private investment in businesses that would otherwise not come into these neighborhoods. Community Development Corporations (CDCs) were created in order to manage the process. But as we shall see, the same mistakes made by the poverty program were repeated here.

On face value, the successes of the CDCs appear impressive. In a *New York Times* op-ed piece, Michael Rubinger, the current chief executive of Local Initiative Service Corporation (LISC), calls for a continuation of the federal tax credits supporting their operations. But Howard Hussock, a national expert on public housing, writes in a summer 2001 *City Journal* article "Don't Let CDCs Fool You" that

> The real worry focuses on the people who actually live in CDC housing. Just like old-fashioned public housing projects, the new subsidized accommodation mostly houses single mothers, who are the main recipients of the Section 8 rent subsidies on which CDC financing relies. (Only 8 percent of households receiving rent vouchers are families with children with both spouses present.) In other words, rather than being an authentic breakthrough in building healthy communities for working families, CDCs are just part of the vast financial support system for illegitimacy, with all its bad effects for both mothers and their children.

Because CDC staffers misunderstand the reason their tenants are poor—blaming supposed injustices in the economic system rather than the bad life decisions of welfare mothers—they're involved in preserving the old welfare culture that the 1996 welfare reforms have begun to supersede.

Further, the arrogance and know-it-allness of the organizers was astounding. Over the years there was an interest in having America Works partner with one of LISC's Community Development affiliates. Their reason was that although they would renovate the housing, within seven years it would return to a dilapidated state because the people living there didn't have the money to sustain it. During the 1990s we visited a number of LISC-sponsored housing projects in Chicago and Indianapolis but never found the right partner. An expansion of welfare-to-work in New York City finally provided the opportunity.

The Human Resources Administration wanted welfare-to-work vendors to have a series of subcontracts with a variety of community services. This was done to placate the nonprofits who were not large enough or well-financed enough to be a prime vendor but could still be supportive. The CDC we selected was converting an old hospital in the south Bronx to low-income housing. In addition, they were providing a full array of training programs, business incubators, and other service. We established the America Works program, hired and trained the director and staff, provided the space, and gave them 50 percent of the profits. Their main focus was not on the job placement of welfare recipients but in having neighborhood residents come to use their industrial kitchens to create products which they could sell and thereby create "businesses." The women who ran the program had very luxurious offices on the top floor. All were white middle-class professionals. They never attended meetings or had involvement with the programs downstairs. If there was a community board it was invisible. The actual board was made up of people living in the suburbs. But financially, the CDC did very well.

As recently as 2011, the budget for this site with about hundred apartments is $10 million a year. The director makes over $200,000 a year. The building is subsidized by section 8 housing and the higher-than-average rents are paid by the taxpayers. These subsidized the staff on the top floor that does PR, fundraising, proposal writing, and so on. The main program that remains is Head Start. We knew from experience that their business incubator programs do not work, but they are very attractive sounding to possible funders.

So here we have a present-day War on Poverty program disguised by fancy financing being foisted on the public as the new way to help the poor. Hussock ends by urging Congress

> to begin doing everything they can do to bring inner-city neighborhoods into the mainstream economy. They should put time limits on the Section 8 rental vouchers that are the CDCs' lifeblood, and so try to weaken the movement. And they should encourage and help cities to spark revival the old-fashioned ways: by providing safe streets, effective schools, attractive parks, and work-oriented, values-laden social programs. Cities must help themselves, too, by controlling costs, lowering taxes, minimizing regulation, and encouraging private housing and commercial development. Shortcuts like CDCs are doomed to be dead ends."[20]

In his opposing op-ed, Rubinger ends by saying, "if these credits were to disappear, so too would billions of annual investment in America's poorest zip codes. The result would be lost jobs, more homelessness, a decimated affordable housing market and decimated communities."[21] The trouble with this argument is that despite the billions pumped into these neighborhoods by LISC, the problems he cites have gotten worse since LISC's inception. We have seen dependency skyrocket, out-of-wedlock births soar, and economic development stumble. As with the original poverty programs, paternalistic benevolence has led to broken promises. Perhaps only with the reform of welfare have we seen a reduction in poverty and an increase in work participation by the recipients. But welfare does not cover all who are poor.

It is startling, having been immersed in the War on Poverty since 1965, that one man, Mitchell Sviridoff, had such an impact on the way we fought the war—and still does. From CPI in New Haven, through the establishment of the Economic Opportunity Act in 1964, the creation of MDRC, PPV, LISC, and the many programs he funded at the Ford Foundation, his imprimatur is huge. When I first got to know him I was in awe of his intelligence and commitment. He funded a program of mine to place mentally retarded people into real jobs. I was certain that his legacy would be one hailed as virtuous and substantial. Among many, I am sure his methods are still hailed. But for me, I now can see the gigantic flaws in his and my vision of helping the poor. They are emblematic of our continued misdiagnosis of the maladies in our society and the means we establish to cure them. Mike did the right thing first—he asked a basic question: why are the poor poor? Sadly, once he decided that society was to blame, he took the wrong road and he was, sadly, not alone.

But Mike's impact on programs is not all negative. I have been influenced by programs like the National Supported Work Demonstration. I ran two of their programs. The lessons

I learned, which were criticized by MDRC, came from our redesigning the program to be more entrepreneurial. MDRC did not respect our placing people in private companies and charging them for the services. But this worked superbly to get people employed, and generated income. This policy initiative would lead to the establishment of America Works' entrepreneurial model.

The National Demonstration was built on the model created by the Vera Institute of Justice. That model and VERA's reliance on muscular research is what has helped America Works place hundreds of thousands of poor people into jobs around the country. With some exceptions, well-intended efforts on the part of many to mitigate poverty and help the poor have too often resulted in only marginal improvements, cost ineffectiveness, and outright failure. As a result, untested theories and programs become sacred, and research gaps remain abound. This has left the country with mostly a failed War on Poverty despite an enormous expenditure of resources. The political process also props up failed programs operated by special interest partners and continues to stymie worthwhile efforts to help the poor. Growing political correctness also muffles necessary candor about issues of personal responsibility, growing numbers of single-parent-headed households, absent fathers, and the importance of all work as a stepping stone out of poverty.

## Notes

1.  Charles Murray, *Losing Ground* (New York: Basic Books, 1984).
2.  Nathan Glazer, *The Limits of Social Policy* (Cambridge, MA: Harvard University Press, 1988).
3.  Michael Puma, *Head Start Research: Third Grade Follow-up to the Head Start Impact Study*, OPRE, 2012, http://www.acf.hhs.gov/sites/default/files/opre/head_start_executive_summary.pdf.
4.  Peter Z. Schochet, John Burghardt, and Sheena McConnell, "Does Job Corps Work? Impact Findings from the National Job

Corps Study," *American Economic Review* 98, no. 5 (December 2008): 1864–86.

5.  Rachel Greszler, Social Security Disability Insurance Trust Fund Will Be Exhausted in Just Two Years: Beneficiaries Facing Nearly 20 Percent Cut in Benefits. The Heritage Foundation, 2014. http://www.heritage.org/research/reports/2014/08/social-security-disability-insurance-trust-fund-will-be-exhausted-in-just-two-years-beneficiaries-facing-nearly-20-percent-cut-in-benefits.

6.  Chana Joffe-Walt, *Unfit for Work: The Startling Rise of Disability in America*, NPR, 2013, http://apps.npr.org/unfit-for-work/.

7.  Dana Sauchelli and Rich Calder, "LIRR Retirees Found Guilty of Faking Disabilities," *New York Post*, October 10, 2013, http://nypost.com/2013/10/10/lirr-retirees-found-guilty-of-faking-disabilities/.

8.  Ibid.

9.  Alexander, "Welfare's Failure."

10. http://www.budget.senate.gov/democratic/public/_cache/files/920da599-e6a4-4a6c-93ca-e4dec6da40db/gary-alexander.pdf; http://legis.wisconsin.gov/senate/darling/PressReleases/Documents/Welfare%20Benefit%20Report.pdf.

11. Casey B. Mulligan, *The Redistribution Recession: How Labor Market Distortions Contracted the Economy* (New York: Oxford University Press, 2012).

12. Michael D. Tanner and Charles Hughes, *The Work versus Welfare Tradeoff: 2013* (Washington, DC: Cato Institute, August 19, 2013).

13. Bruce Berg, *New York City Politics: Governing Gotham* (New York: Rutgers University Press, 2007), 173.

14. G. Waddell and A. K. Burton AK, *Is Work Good for Your Health and Well-Being?* (London: The Stationery Office, 2006).

15. Alexis de Tocqueville, *Democracy in America* (New York: Vintage Books, 1990), Vol. II, 1990, p. 106.

16. http://www.brookings.edu/blogs/social-mobility-memos/posts/2015/05/06-moving-to-opportunity-revisited-rothwell.

17. Cindy Redcross, Megan Millenky, Timothy Rudd, and Valerie Levshin, *More Than a Job: Final Results from the Evaluation of the Center for Employment Opportunities (CEO) Transitional Jobs Program* (Washington, DC: Administration for Children and

Families, U.S. Department of Health and Human Services, 2012), figure ES-1.

18. Ibid., tables ES-1, ES-3.

19. Ibid., ES-6, ES-18.

20. Howard Husock, "Don't Let CDCs Fool You," *City Journal,* Summer 2001, http://www.city-journal.org/html/11_3_dont_let_cdcs.html.

21. Michael Rubinger, "Two Tax Credits That Work," *New York Times,* July 12, 2013, http://www.nytimes.com/2013/07/13/opinion/two-tax-credits-that-work.html?_r=0.

# 5

# America Works: Policy Implications for Dependency and Poverty Reduction

*"Wishful thinking is not sound public policy."*

—Bjorn Lomborg[1]

In 1984 I established America Works, the first for-profit welfare-to-work company in the United States. Lee helped with the establishment as a consultant and quickly joined the company to assume the position of CEO. At the time I was sitting on the board of a nonprofit along with some young businessmen who encouraged me to take our model on the road. Of course, the only viable way to do this was through investment capital to fund the venture. I used some of my own money and borrowed the remainder from a bank to start the enterprise. I secured a grant from Ohio, where Governor Dick Celeste had encouraged us to enter and run a welfare-to-work program.

Governor Celeste was unhappy at the time with the way the county welfare offices were performing. He was willing to spend some political capital to go against them and try something different to reduce welfare dependency. But the counties ended up having more power than Celeste could foresee. Those entrenched welfare interests ultimately convinced the legislature to cancel our contracts and reclaim the money for themselves.

Politics plays an outsized role hand in the survival of my business. More often than not, politics gets in the way, and this undermines those we are trying to help.

One thing to point out about America Works is that from the beginning we saw it as a vehicle both for operating programs and for conducting research—the latter to make certain, as Rabbi Heschel advised, that we "knew what we saw." I had learned from Herb Sturtz at the Vera Institute of Justice that research, preferably in the form of controlled, experimental studies, had the best chance of influencing public officials. This was the model he originated and that I endeavored to replicate. I was adamant that we had to be evidence-based—not just to justify our existence but because we wished to do the most good. All our competitors sold themselves solely on their compassion and willingness to help. And unfortunately, when some welfare companies like Seedco do employ self-reporting, they can cook the books to support the program. For instance, in 2012, renegade staff at Seedco reported hundreds to thousands of fake job placements to New York City in order to obtain $8 million in performance-based pay.[2] Too often we fall into the trap of thinking that since we want to do good and we are acting to do good, we must be doing something good, right? Yet we have seen how often this is not the case when it comes to results. Instead, our program would define success by real, measurable outcomes, not benevolent inputs.

What Lee and I have done with America Works is to constantly turn a critical eye on our own program and evaluate its effectiveness. Based on our assessment of its results, we would then alter or jettison each individual approach. This may sound like simple common sense, but the unfortunate reality is that objective self-review and recalibration are rarely the norm with most social programs. The widespread belief that commitment, good intentions, and good deeds are enough carries the day. Politicians love this since they can support programs in return for votes without having to worry about whether they work or not. There is little enthusiasm for rigorous research or clear-eyed analysis. Accountability would just get in the way.

We first delved into research-driven programs in our early welfare-to-work efforts. For example, in the early 1990s, in preparation for the coming welfare reforms, we conducted reviews of our nonprofit programs in Massachusetts and found that investing into jobs would reduce welfare expenditures by five times. The State Senate's then-Chair of Ways and Means, Chet Atkins, understood the potential savings to the Commonwealth and initiated a statewide program expanding on our model. We used data from these programs and others to form our theories on how to reduce welfare dependency and to help mold the welfare act of 1996, which made work-first central to the new welfare reform.

America Works continued to build off these experiences. We were encouraged to mount prisoner-to-work programs and then evaluate them to see if they would really do what we believed they could. We did this throughout the country, from Oakland, CA, to New York City. Initial research by William B. Eimicke and Steven Cohen suggested that it might well reduce recidivism.[3] At that time, discussions with the Manhattan Institute in New York City began a dialogue around what we called the missing men—the fathers and others who were either not with their families or were incarcerated. The Manhattan Institute decided with us that a control/experimental study would answer the question definitively.

We were encouraged by our results up to then in the eight programs we have run. As noted earlier from state to state, the recidivism rate for people we have placed in jobs has been from 4 percent to 8 percent, while a statewide figure of 30–35 percent is not uncommon. A new Manhattan Institute study now gives a definitive answer to the question whether work reduces recidivism to crime. A randomized trial was conducted involving 259 ex-offenders in New York City, all of whom had been released from prison, jail, or a youth correctional facility within six months of the study. Only 31.1 percent of nonviolent offenders who received America Works job placement were rearrested during the eighteen to thirty-six months that followed. In contrast, those who received standard job training, currently offered by the state (and mainly oriented toward education and self-directed job searches), were rearrested at a rate of 50 percent. The program estimated that the cost of the America Works program would be $5000 per client, yielding an average savings of about $231,000 for each nonviolent ex-offender, not to mention the incalculable benefits to society of averted crimes. The Manhattan Institute and America Works will work to publicize the results through conferences and briefings of legislators in states and in Washington. We will push for a redirection of criminal justice funds from strategies that do not work to those that create jobs for returning offenders. The reduction in crime and its attendant cost savings should begin to attract government interest with budgets as tight as they are now.[4]

Now we have even further proof that work reduces recidivism to crime and fast attachment to the workplace is the best strategy.[5] The Manhattan Institute and the Smith Richardson Foundation published a study in 2015 that answers definitively whether work reduces recidivism to crime. The paper's key finding is that training designed to quickly place former inmates in jobs decreases the likelihood that ex-offenders with nonviolent histories will be rearrested by 20 percent.[6]

The lessons we have learned at America Works can be broken down into public policy recommendations and some general guidelines for the effective operations of programs aimed at reducing dependency. Of course, many in our field will challenge some or all of these recommendations. Nevertheless, I stand firmly on these because they have worked in over a dozen cities. Not only that, they've worked with many different populations, from welfare recipients, ex-offenders, veterans, physically and emotionally handicapped people, to teens aging out of the foster care system, and single fathers. Experience proves that the America Works techniques are successful—from small-scale pilot programs, like one which placed hundreds of New Yorkers with HIV into stable jobs, to larger initiatives, such as America Works' network of companies that has placed 4492 homeless veterans into jobs since 2009. Unfortunately, it is impossible to get comparable figures from other providers of similar services. What can be said is that this is a very difficult population to place into jobs—drugs and PTSD are a few of the common barriers. To have placed over 4000 homeless vets into jobs is impressive by any standards.

Arguments challenging the effectiveness of our approach are invariably based upon ideology and politics, rather than facts. Bowes and I have tried to fight for the adoption of many of our philosophies, particularly work-first and pay for performance, at the national and local levels. Where we do training, it is very targeted to what the industry or company managers tell us they would like to see. While we have had limited success, there is continuing opposition from the government and the welfare-industrial complex. In fact, under the Obama administration education and training has taken once again preeminence in welfare reduction despite its proven, disappointing results in the past.[7]

And so, here for review are my practical, road-tested recommendations for mounting work programs for the poor.

## Work-First

Much has already been written in this book about work-first—America Works' core policy of placing clients directly into work and then using education and training to upgrade them. When I entered the War on Poverty, the prevailing policy for employment programs was to use education and training to develop human capital as the quickest route back to employment. It had worked for the programs' planners, so why should it not for low-income-dependent people? The answer, we found, was that many of our clients had been failed by education and training systems before they ever got to us. To put them back into the classroom made no sense. They had been failed by public education. They had been led astray or taken advantage of by community programs in many cases having paid proprietary institutions for skills they could not market. Often they were encouraged to take loans that they could not afford. And the programs! Training for nonexistent jobs. "Training," as Lee says, "by poor teachers, of poor programs for poor people." Clients were unable to visualize any benefits that would accrue from more time spent sitting and listening to people who they had no reason to trust. But the poverty program elite, satisfied to plan from above and never visit any actual programs, had no idea that their experiences did not translate.

Bowes and I ran many education and training programs that were unsuccessful before turning to programs that prioritized job placement. The benefits of quick reentry into the labor force were immediate. People gained confidence from witnessing that employers wanted them. They had been paid so long *not* to work that they hardly believed anyone would want them.

It was clear that having been failed by these programs for so long, putting clients back in a classroom tended to reinforce their belief that they were never going to get a job. So we devised the "work first, education later" model. Having been rejected for jobs in the past, why not give them an initial success to build upon? Then use education and training to upgrade. And that made sense to most. Working next to someone who was doing the same job but making 50 cents more because they had a high school degree, a high school equivalency program suddenly became more attractive.

As a side note, we began to notice an interesting phenomenon among many of our clients. Welfare recipients would often come in and give excuses as to why they could not work. A frequent reason cited was the lack of daycare for their young children. We would send them out on interviews anyway and most often they would quickly be hired by willing employers. As if by magic, once they had been placed in a job, daycare would materialize in the form of relatives, friends, or local daycare providers. What was happening here is clear. They were insecure about their prospects and used the most convenient excuse to make themselves unavailable for work. Once presented with the prospect of a job, their confidence grew and the perceived barriers were overcome.

## Performance-Based Contracting

One of the key tenants of America Works is our belief in paying for results. We've already seen that agencies like those that executed the War on Poverty aren't big advocates of empirical research. Part of the same mindset is their tendency to demand payment for expenses, rather than upon successful accomplishment of their objective. Performance-based contracting forces accountability. This is demanded of other government contractors—just imagine having to pay full contract price if Boeing delivered only half of the airplanes contracted for—yet for some reason is abandoned when discussing welfare. We could not understand why the government paid for finished products in other arenas, such as pencils or airplanes, but refused to do the same for placing and keeping people in jobs and off government dependence.

Until the 1900s, the principal format of a government contract was one that paid for line items. This meant that you were reimbursed for the expenses you submitted in the budget portion of your proposal. Regardless of the success of the program, payment was made so long as you could prove that you spent the money on approved items. The object of any program operator, then, was to maximize revenue by spending as much as possible, rather than focusing on achieving your stated goals.

Because America Works was the first organization to deliver welfare-to-work services as a for-profit enterprise—an unpleasant combination for some—it was incumbent on us to display real success and taxpayer accountability. We designed our contracts so that the government would pay us only if a person was placed in a job, stayed employed for a minimum amount of time, and either moved off welfare or had his grant substantially reduced.

Since we are paid only for our results, our staff is held accountable for their clients' successes—which means identifying companies with appropriate jobs, placing people in them, and then keeping them in those jobs. They are compensated as they do this just as we in upper management are. This system both motivates our staff and creates a culture of accountability, ensuring that our companies, the clients, and the taxpayer all get what they are paying for.

One need only compare our performance with our competitors to see that our system must work. We, as a company, are paid for performance. Therefore, our staff knows that they must perform or we would go out of business. Rewards for competition drive performance. This has worked well for us, and it is why we are regularly rated the best performer by New York City's government.[8]

There is still great resistance to this, particularly in the nonprofit world but also among many of our for-profit competitors. And believe it or not, government agencies like the US Department of Labor still shy away from true pay-for-performance. Why? There are two major reasons. First, most programs are more comfortable being reimbursed for their expenses and not risking financial losses if they do not place enough people in jobs. The liberal bent is to see the clients as damaged and victims, and who would want *them* as your measure of potential success? Better keep them at arm's length and not be rewarded for their performance, which is likely to fail. Second, politicians prefer to support community organizations and for-profit providers who will support them, quid pro quo. Exposing the effectiveness of the groups makes it harder to continue funding these inefficient programs.

In our field, we talk a lot about "best practices" when trying to improve our programs' successes. I will say unequivocally that there is only one best practice—and that is paying for results. I challenge other program operators to prove me wrong. This is competition and capitalism at its best. The government sets the terms of who shall be served and how much it is worth, and the marketplace develops the tools to deliver. In the words of Steve Savas, the grandfather of privatization, here the government steers, and the marketplace rows.

Before leaving this critical policy lesson, there is one point that needs to be amplified. The potential to make or lose money is a central element of our market-driven society. People drawn to government tend to be mistrustful of the private for-profit sectors. Yet it is this economic principle that has powered our preeminence in the world. As I commented earlier, capitalism has taken more people out of poverty throughout the world than any other economic system. Instead of government bureaucrats cooking up new flavor-of-the-month program designs, they should be thinking the following: what is our objective, what is it worth, and why not allow both nonprofits and, yes, for-profit companies propose their solutions, to be paid only when the objective is achieved? Those goals should be the success of the endeavor, not milestones along the way.

### Work Is a Magic Bullet

One of the most important discoveries we have made at America Works is that work not only reduces recidivism to crime, but is also the most effective antidote to all sorts of other public and personal problems.[9]

For example, America Works received a grant from the Ford Foundation to help establish a small pilot program placing mentally challenged individuals from sheltered workshops into jobs. It was startling to see how their "workshop behavior"—rocking back and forth, wearing silly hats, and so on—changed as the workplace socialized them. Until we came along, the best workers had been kept in the sheltered workshops since they were the most productive. We found that they, and many of their fellow workers, responded favorably to a normal environment and the demands of the workplace.[10]

Work has also worked for veterans, a group in which America Works has invested much effort and substantial resources. Veterans face unique challenges finding work upon returning to civilian life, due to their higher rates of disability and lack of work experience outside the military, among other hurdles. The unemployment rate among those who have served since 9/11 is 10 percent, with two hundred and forty-six thousand out of work.[11] We have placed 4492 homeless veterans in jobs since 2009. Work works, and each time we substitute social work, therapy, and social services for the primacy of work we subvert our objectives of reducing poverty, deviance, and dependency.

## Most Want to Work but the Government Discourages Them

In late July 2013, then Representative Steve Southerland from Florida visited the America Works location in Washington. I had cowritten an op-ed column with him supporting his bill for work requirements for food stamp recipients. He is a compassionate conservative. His family has long operated a funeral home in Panama City, FL, which serves poor people and gives free burials from time to time to those who cannot afford the service. I told the Congressman the story about Giuliani and when he emerged from listening to the stories of the people there, he said, "You know, there was a bit of Rudy's skepticism in me when I went in. I see what he saw, which was the desire by them for work."

As noted earlier, in some areas the government incentives are so poorly designed that the amount of total income gained by not working may well exceed that for work. However, and this is always missed by economists and other commentators, most people would rather work than sit at home and collect government handouts. The psychological and social benefits often outweigh the drop in the total income provided by the state.

Sure, there are other programs to get people working, and a few of them actually work. But except for the federal welfare reforms of 1996, most programs ultimately still encourage continued dependence. As previously mentioned, in 2013, New York City was told by the Department of Agriculture to stop requiring food stamp recipients to work as a condition of continued support, even though it is required by the Personal Responsibility and Work Opportunity Act of 1996. Social Security disability claims are rising at an alarming rate (even as our health care improves), and conditions are still in place that assure many more people will be granted disability payments that they do not need. Federal administrative judges deciding on SSDI cases are forced into a rigid checkbox called the vocational grid that uses all sorts of irrelevant factors in deciding who is eligible. The federal government established the grid to guide the judges in applying criteria for disability fairly and impartially. For example, if you had done physical work there is no expectation that you could do a desk job. If you are older, you are not expected to do physical labor. Sensible enough—but the grid also bizarrely accounts for whether or not the recipient speaks English. According to economists Mark Warshawsky and Ross Marchand, "at age 50 a person who can perform only sedentary work and is completely unskilled is presumptively disabled. A 49-year-old is not, unless he or she cannot speak English. The non-English-speaker, limited to sedentary work, is disabled. This rule results in the payment of benefits to non-English-speakers in Puerto Rico despite the fact that the common language there is Spanish." The result is that people receive disability benefits, even though they can and should work.[12]

### Tax Credits to Encourage Hiring Do Not Work, But Wage Supplementation Does

In order to put people to work, you need employers willing to hire them. America Works has discovered that the best route to encouraging hiring is not tax credits but wage supplementation. Yet politicians regularly recommend offering tax credits to companies to encourage hiring of disadvantaged populations. I remember being with then President Clinton on New Year's Day in 1997. Bowes and I came down for coffee bleary-eyed from the night before when Bill and Hillary had spent an hour answering questions off the record, followed by late-night New Year's Eve partying. It was 10 AM and Bill bounced into the breakfast room already having completed nine holes of golf. He approached us and said, "You know, there should be an America Works in every city in America." I thanked him, at which point he began a five-minute policy exposition on welfare and how tax credits were working to get welfare recipients hired. I listened, knowing that our experience had actually confirmed the ineffectiveness of them, but I was too awed by his magnetic presence to offer a rebuttal.

Despite President Clinton's monumental reform of welfare he was wrong about this—tax credits do not work. Managers are seeking good, steady, trainable workers. They understandably believe that if you are attaching a tax incentive to a disadvantaged person you are sticking them with a problem. On top of that, tax credits take months or even years to collect. For those companies operating with tight margins, this is no incentive at all. While the idea of a tax incentive seems like a good idea, in practice it fails miserably. As scholar Rebecca Blank writes, the targeted jobs tax credit (TJTC) is "available to employers who hire low-wage workers from certain target groups. Employers' taxes can be reduced by up to $2,400 per worker, essentially subsidizing the wages paid to these workers and theoretically making it more attractive for employers to hire them. Most employers who could collect on the TJTC do not, and there is evidence that eligibility for such programs stigmatizes workers in the labor market rather than helping them. There is little research evidence that the TJTC has stimulated increases in the employment of disadvantaged workers." In my experience, at best, companies go back, look at their hires, and then apply for a tax break that had no effect on their hiring.[13]

On-the-job training money has also been available for decades from the federal and some state governments. It has generally failed to make much headway in encouraging them to employ targeted populations. The red tape and the requirement that there be a guarantee of employment at the end of training have made employers wary of entering into contracts. As will be seen here, there is a way to do this—wage supplementation. Does this mean all on-the-job training is useless? Of course not, just as all education and training is not useless. It is that the majority of efforts in both cases have failed to be employer sensitive and have been operated by less-than-competent organizations.

We have found the best way to encourage hiring is wage supplementation. During the stimulus under President Obama, a small amount of money was designated to supplement wages for employers who hired disadvantaged workers. This in effect created a trial job period to evaluate the individual's performance. America Works designed our program to be company-friendly. No contracts requiring hiring of the workers. No red tape. Each month, upon the submission of a time sheet, America Works staff would issue a check for between 25 percent and 75 percent of the worker's salary. No waiting months for checks from the government, just an offset to wages. Most we placed were hired after the supplemental wages ran out. And just as important, because of the additional income from us, some companies created two jobs instead of one. In late February 2016, the *New York Times* led with an editorial in its Sunday edition calling for a substantial increase in funding for employment subsidy programs to counter high minority unemployment. The New York Times noted that a nonprofit organization called the Economic Mobility Corporation had analyzed the stimulus package's outcomes in four states. The *Times* summed up the report's findings: "By subsidizing the hiring of temporary employees the federal Government lowered labor costs and kept some employers afloat through the recession."[14]

## Guidelines for Effective Management of Programs to Reduce Dependency

A successful program needs a professional, businesslike approach based on mutual respect. The client is there because we assume they want a job and the agency, America Works, respects that and seeks to meet that goal. Without those parameters there is no partnership.

*Respect for the Clients*

When Bowes and I and our partner Abe Levovitz bought and took over a failing America Works copycat company called New York Works, Bowes found a remarkable clause in their lease in Astor Place. It prohibited welfare clients from being trained onsite. We were absolutely mystified. These were their clients, whom they were to serve. It was like a New York deli not being allowed to sell bagels. What was going on here?

It quickly became clear that the program operators neither believed in their clients nor wished to mingle with them. How foolish and doomed to failure. And what a typical expression of liberal program design hypocrisy.

Into this dysfunctional world came America Works and Bowes, as CEO, turned this behavior and belief system on its head. First, the offices were required to maintain a corporate atmosphere. Most programs to this day have operating space that is sloppy and unprofessional, showing a total disregard for the clients. America Works built offices that showed we respected the clients. Second, our staff dressed professionally—ties, jackets, and dresses. Third, a deep social commitment was required of staff. These elements translated into programs that were both caring and effective. Our clients are frequently telling us that they are being treated with kindness and respect—something missing in other programs they have attended.

Respect is a prerequisite for success of our program since, being paid for performance, the client must be satisfied or they will go elsewhere. This is no problem for a program paid for its expenses, but death to us if we lose people and cannot place them. In part, this is the genius of being paid for outcomes.

*Sales-Driven Staff*

The world of "manpower programs" is staffed by "job developers." In truth, they do not develop jobs; only economic development and investment of private capital develop jobs. What they do is search for already existing job openings and refer people to these. Often they would have the clients conduct these searches themselves. Rudimentary "job banks" would be devised, usually with listings for jobs already filled or with no intention of being filled from the outside.

At America Works, we did not have that luxury. Real jobs that were open and appropriate for each client were mandatory since, again, we were only paid if the client obtained and was retained in a job for some time. Bowes' answer was to create a professional sales force quite like that in the staffing industry. This meant hard-driving, bottom-line salespeople who went out into the field, met with line managers, and sought the right person to fill the position. It meant scoping out the work environment and matching the right person to the job.

The sales teams were paid a salary but were paid incentives for their performance just as we were. The more people successfully placed in jobs, the more compensation they got. This drove performance and efficiency, something quite unusual in programs without performance contracts.

*Placing in Jobs Is the Easy Part*

Most employment programs for the disadvantaged operate with a dump-them-and-run attitude. The goal is placement. Retention was not paid for and so it was not a priority. At America Works, our job only begins when our clients get a job. Bowes created a position called the corporate representative to ensure that every good worker got the support they needed to keep their job. Most clients do not have strong social networks to help with what I call the static in their lives—an abusive mate, lost daycare or housing, difficulty learning the mores of the workplace, and other impediments to holding a job. Bowes observes that people don't so much lose their jobs for what they do not know, but for their inability to fit in. Our mission is to be one step ahead of the line manager and intervene where necessary in all this static to save the client's job. Again, this comes from the brilliance of pay-for-performance, which forces us to come up with strategies that will maximize clients' success and consequently our revenue.

*Rigorous Controls and Monitoring*

We are audited for the placements we claim and the time our clients are retained in their jobs. The internal controls for this are critical. Staff get paid for claiming placements and we must make certain that these happened. Any requests for payment for placements not made can be subject to charges of fraud. This is quite different from the usual pay-for-expenses controls and has necessitated creative management techniques to accomplish systemic and honest accountability. In fact, Lee has worked with governments to help them create effective monitoring protocols. Perhaps the major changes in our programs based on our own and others' assessments were to reduce education and training, replace work-first as the first strike in getting people off dependency, and modify the education and training to better move people up in their jobs. (See Chapter 6.)

Some of these lessons will help guide government policy. Others might teach program operators how to more effectively manage their programs and what to advocate to government officials. Our placing hundreds of thousands of people into jobs is a direct result of following these guiding principles. Proposing work instead of welfare is a direct result of my firsthand experience with work-first. As we move to solutions to poverty, these lessons will be embedded in all of the strategies I suggest.

## Notes

1.  http://www.nationalreview.com/article/224474/dont-freak-out-interview.
2.  Michael Powell, "U.S. Files Suit Against Jobs Agency Used by City," *The New York Times*, May 22, 2012. Web. January 19, 2015.
3.  William B. Eimicke and Steven Cohen, "America Works' Criminal Justice Program: Providing Second Chances Through Work," *Civic Bulletin* 29 (November 2002). http://dx.doi.org/10.7916/D89W0D2N.
4.  A. Yelowitz and C. Bollinger, "Prison-To-Work: The Benefits of Intensive Job-Search Assistance for Former Inmates," Manhattan Institute for Policy Research, Civic Report No. 96, March 2015.
5.  Ibid.
6.  http://www.manhattan-institute.org/html/cb_51.htm.
7.  Stephanie Condon, "Obama: Skills and Training as Valuable as College Degree," CBSNews. CBS Interactive, January 30, 2014. Web. July 14, 2015; Career Pathways. New York: City of

New York, 2014. Nyc.gov. The City of New York, November 1, 2014. Web. July 14, 2015.

8.  See Figure 1, Introduction, of this book.

9.  See note 137 above. On the positive effects of work on different hard-to-employ groups, see http://www.acf.hhs.gov/sites/default/files/opre/tj_09_paper_embed.pdf, p. 5, table 1.

10. http://www.acf.hhs.gov/sites/default/files/opre/tj_09_paper_embed.pdf, p. 43.

11. http://www.washingtonpost.com/blogs/wonkblog/wp/2013/11/11/recent-veterans-are-still-experiencing-double-digit-unemployment/.

12. http://mercatus.org/sites/default/files/Warshawsky-SSDI-Eligibility-Criteria.pdf.

13. Rebecca M. Blank, "The Employment Strategy: Public Policies to Increase Work and Earnings," in *Confronting Poverty: Prescriptions for Change*, eds. Sheldon H. Danziger, Gary D. Sandefur, and Daniel H. Weinberg (New York: Russell Sage Foundation, and Cambridge, MA: Harvard University Press, 1994), 195.

14. "The Crisis of Minority Unemployment," *The New York Times*, 20 Feb. 2016. Web. 10 Aug. 2016.

# 6

# Education and Training versus Work-First

*"Work banishes those three great evils, boredom, vice and poverty"*

—Voltaire[1]

*"I hold a little fundraiser every day. Its called going to work."*

—Stephen Colbert

Getting a job, if you are able-bodied, is a crucial first step to success for multiple reasons inherent to American culture. This chapter looks at the many benefits of work and explores a significant body of research, which clearly states that entering the first rung in the labor force as rapidly as possible is a tried and true strategy for advancement. Employment not only is the best avenue to economic security, but also makes you an important, positive, adult role model for children, you continually develop new skills, learn new things, and build a record of employment that can lead to a better job and further education or skill training in the future.

There are innumerable arguments for working rather than receiving welfare. The most obvious is simple: work is a very effective way to reduce poverty. Work provides far more money than government assistance. It is also far more stable and recession-resistant. A recent AEI-Brookings report remarked upon this fact—when more people are working, even during an economic downturn like the Great Recession of 2008, the poverty rate does not sink so low as when greater numbers of people are reliant on government support.[2]

Work also improves the worker's state of mind. Several studies show that poor people feel better about themselves when they work. One study asked recipients of welfare whether they had any ability to change the important things in their life: 31.8 percent of unemployed welfare recipients admitted that they felt little ability to change their lives, while only 17.9 percent of those employed full-time agreed with such a statement. This suggests that work is vital to happiness.[3]

Holding a job is far healthier than not. As we explored in Chapter 3, researchers have demonstrated strong links between unemployment and increased mortality rates, greater susceptibility to respiratory infections, and increased rates of cardiovascular disease, lung cancer, and suicide.[4] Meanwhile, a recent review of the scholarly literature on work found a broad consensus that work can even be healthful for the sick and disabled, since work "is therapeutic, helps to promote recovery and rehabilitation, leads to better health outcomes, minimizes the deleterious physical, mental, and social side effects of long-term sickness absence and worklessness," among other positives.[5]

Most interestingly, work generates public support for anti-poverty policies. Public opinion studies stress that the public insists that employable adults work if they are to get serious assistance from government. Indeed, the public will to enforce work is much stronger than the will to limit spending on the poor. To the contrary, the public supports even increased spending if it will move the nonworking poor into employment.[6]

Perhaps the best indicator of the importance of work can be found in the dire consequences for people who have none. According to the *Los Angeles Times*, "Nearly 12% of Americans between ages 18 and 25 were deemed to be depressed based on their answers to eight questions that were part of a survey conducted by the Centers for Disease Control and Prevention and state health departments. But within this age group, those who were unemployed were 3.17 times more likely to be depressed than their counterparts with jobs. . . . Depression during these formative years can have 'long-term consequences,' they wrote, including setting people up for a lifetime of lower earnings."[7]

To a degree, the government pitches in to support people with low-paying jobs, making sure that they're able to access the positive effects of work, even if their wages are not high enough to lift them out of poverty. Working at low or modest wages makes you eligible for generous wage supplements through the tax system such as the earned income tax credit (EITC) and the child tax credit that add substantial dollars to your actual earnings. In many states you are also likely eligible for subsidized child care.[8] Your first job might not be the type of job you want forever, but it will build your resume and give you skills you can use to move upward and start a career. In the words of Martin Luther King, Jr., "No work is insignificant. All labor that uplifts humanity has dignity and importance and should be undertaken with painstaking excellence."

The real question at hand, however, is whether the norms that applied in the past are still applied now to able-bodied adults on welfare. Based on my experiences and on crunching the hard data, I would argue that for years our cash welfare system diminished the value of work and increased dependence on government for many adults, predominantly single parent women. Only since 1988, when a first real attempt to encourage work for those on welfare was undertaken by the Family Support Act—Job Opportunity and Basic Skills (JOBS) program, has the country begin to tilt, albeit slowly, toward a true work-based and personal responsibility approach to welfare reform. The 1996 Personal Responsibility and Work Opportunity Reconciliation Act, by creating TANF, greatly accelerated the new norm as cash assistance being temporary and work or activities preparatory to work being expected.

This shift came predominantly for three reasons:

1) Americans believe in work and expect people who are able-bodied to work;
2) More and more women entered the labor market beginning in the 1960s and continue to do so today, making single mothers on welfare the outliers instead of the norm;
3) The advent of new wage supplement programs such as the EITC and other tax credits made it indisputable that having a job makes people far better off economically than remaining on welfare.

Ron Haskins, a former White House and congressional advisor on welfare issues, sums it up succinctly: "Americans place a high value on adults who work hard to support themselves and their children. As a result any group that becomes known for non-work is, by definition, unequal to working Americans. Government support for non-work exacerbates the problem of social inequality both because it encourages non-work and because productive citizens resent being forced to support those who so conspicuously flout the value Americans place on work and self-support."[9]

Based on the rigorous evaluation of various JOBS Programs begun in 1988 and the pivotal National Evaluation of Welfare to Work Strategies (NEWWS) in the late 1990s and early 2000s, a work-first approach has proven to be a far more effective strategy than a human capital approach. The component study of the NEWWS provides particularly compelling evidence on this point—showing that those in work-first pro-grams were not only more likely to get and keep jobs than those in education-first programs, but earned more money as well. One group of individuals drawn from Portland, OR, averaged $900 more per year than those who hadn't participated in work-first programs, while groups from other cities saw gains of $400–500 per year. In all cases, work-first programs tended to be the most effective at reducing reliance on welfare and increasing reliance on earnings instead.[10]

As Amy Brown states in *A How-to Guide. Work First*: "What defines (work first) programs is their overall philosophy: that any job is a good job and that the best way to succeed in the labor market is to join it, developing work habits and skills on the job rather than in a classroom."[11] In other words the best approach to welfare reform is getting people into an entry-level job and then offering ongoing skill training and education that can and hopefully will lead to a career ladder. In short, "Work is what works."[12]

Even the federal government seems to recognize that work-first works. The hinge moment in the history of the govern-ment's changing relationship to work and welfare came in 1996. That year, the Welfare Reform Act (PRWORA) created TANF and finally made work and personal responsibility the basic underpinnings of the nation's cash welfare system. It imposed penalties on able-bodied recipients who did not comply with new work requirements, placed federal time limits on the receipt of welfare, and imposed penalties on states that did not meet employment goals. It repealed the Aid to Families with Dependent Children program enacted in 1935 as part of the Social Security Act and replaced it with the Temporary Assistance for Needy Families (TANF) Program, which ended the lifetime entitlement to welfare benefits in favor of a tem-porary program in the form of a fixed block grant to states.[13]

The repeal of AFDC was an enormous event that funda-mentally changed the architecture of welfare. Ron Haskins, a major player in drafting the 1996 act when he was staff to the House Ways and Means Committee, described AFDC as "the little acorn, a tiny and inconspicuous program—designed originally to support widows with minor children—(that) grew into the towering oak that is the huge array of federal and federal-state programs designed to provide benefits and services to the poor." Kate O' Beirne (formerly at HHS under Ronald Reagan, then the Heritage Foundation, and now of *National Review*) astutely said in her 1995 welfare reform testimony to the House Ways and Means Committee that the existing system lived on the philosophy of "Spend more and demand less."[14]

Prior to PRWORA, predecessor programs such as the Work Incentive Program (WIN) of 1967 and the JOBS program cre-ated in 1988 as part of the Family Support Act rhetorically stressed work, but did not have strong requirements, strong enforcement tools, or clear expectations of AFDC recipients, instead allowing states to experiment (mostly unsuccessfully) with different approaches.

At least with the JOBS program, due to the seminal research done in 1986 by Professor Lawrence Mead of NYU that proved its effectiveness, congressional Republicans and even some Democrats began to adopt Mead's philosophy that work requirements backed by aggressively run programs should be the central pillar of welfare reform. Mead's studies proved that this approach forced clients to change behaviors and rapidly enter the workforce. This heralded a growing new conviction that "work is what works."[15] Ron Haskins refers to Mead's book as having "immense influence . . . [by arguing] that the poor needed aggressively administered and authoritative welfare programs to force them to adopt appropriate behaviors. The most important such behavior was of course work."[16] The JOBS program thus marked an important milestone on the route to PRWORA in 1996. Slowly, there was a growing consensus that the best course of action would be to reduce welfare caseloads by getting people jobs, and quickly.

In the wake of the welfare reform law, even liberal researchers began to recognize the inexorable shift toward emphasizing work. Referring to the Family Support Act and the JOBS Program, Irene Lurie of the Rockefeller Institute noted: "But the Act emphasized education and training for welfare clients and, perhaps because it deemphasized immediate employment, was ineffective in reducing caseloads."[17]

Despite Mead's work, states ultimately lined up in two camps regarding how to successfully reform what had been a long-standing entitlement program that expected little if anything of recipients and had not stressed work. These two camps have come to define our modern debate over welfare programs.

The first camp, under the lingering liberal bias that the poor needed further education and training before they could work, stressed the old "human capital approach" consisting of often lengthy preparation, continuing education and training, and credential development, that, while well intentioned, was often unrelated to actual labor market needs and available employment. While advanced education and training in many instances can make a difference in longer term higher wages, it is often not the right initial approach for welfare recipients, many of whom have dropped out of school and do not want continuing education, as noted by under-enrollment by able-bodied adults even in voluntary education and training programs when offered. According to one 2002 study, "Few welfare recipients (only 8 percent in some studies) state that they want to go back to school to study reading and math; they have had poor experiences in school in the past and prefer to get specific skills train-ing (around 60 percent) or help looking for a job (about 30 percent)."[18] From this data it's clear that what recipients really want is a job.

The second camp felt very differently, trusting Mead's data that the best avenue to help those on welfare improve their circumstances was rapid attachment to employment, an approach that has come to be known as "work-first." Under work-first, short-term soft skill development is stressed (dress-ing appropriately, respecting authority, assistance with resume preparation, mock interviews, and job search activities) followed by rapid job placement with employers in various sectors including health care, child care, security, hospitality, and retail that consistently hire entry-level workers in both strong and weak economies.

Fortunately, at the time this clash of approaches was taking place, fairly robust funding became available for developing further empirical research to test which approach was most effective as well as what combinations and sequences of ser-vices were likely to yield positive results. Numerous organiza-tions including MDRC (formerly Manpower Demonstration and Research Corporation), Abt Associates, Mathematica Policy Research, and others followed in Mead's footsteps and undertook their own unbiased random assignment studies of many state JOBS programs.[19]

MDRC quickly became a heavyweight in the welfare eval-uation field and produced in 1997 a study of the Riverside California model, where the goal was simple—"get a job, any job." MDRC demonstrated that the Riverside approach increased recipient wages by more than 50 percent, about three times the outcome of other rival programs still empha-sizing education and training in their JOBS programs. This study did more than any other to debunk the long-held theory that training should come before work. Their findings swept the country, establishing a nationwide trend of work-first that by 1997 led almost every state to focus on getting recipients entry-level jobs as a first order of business.[20]

Another important study demonstrating the primacy of work was what's become known as the Bloom, Hill, and Riccio study, which first used innovative multilevel research methods coupled with client surveys to synthesize results from individual MDRC studies.[21] The MDRC studies in individual states demonstrated the superiority of work-first, but often the components of how states implemented these policies differed to some degree. This study effectively aggregated MDRC studies measuring the impact of programs on earnings at fifty-nine local sites. "Their findings clearly state that where a work first/rapid job entry approach was utilized individual impacts were raised by $720 [per year], while human capital/personalized services only raised impacts by $428."[22]

Others came to similar conclusions stating that the two Bloom, Hill and Riccio multilevel analysis studies of 2003 and 2005 proved that "programs that had a stronger emphasis on quick movement into the workforce had much larger earnings impacts than those with a weaker emphasis (and) . . . larger increases in basic education participation were found to be negatively correlated with earnings impacts. . . ."[23]

Published in 2005, the NEWWS was even more thorough in its findings that work-first is a superior approach to human capital education and training.[24] This comprehensive study of eleven programs around the country also found that those stressing labor force attachment outperformed those emphasizing human capital development.[25] NEWWS also looked at a four-year follow-up period and showed that finding employment quickly clearly led to better long-term outcomes: higher wages and longer durations of employment than for those who took longer to start employment.

"Most Successful (worked for over 75 percent of the four-year follow-up period): Members of this group found a job relatively quickly—on average they were unemployed less than half a quarter initially. Least Successful (employed 25 percent or less of the follow-up period): Members of this group experienced the longest spells of initial jobless-ness. They started working well into the follow-up period (i.e. during the second year of follow-up period)."[26] These findings were a major reason why national policy now demands that states running welfare emphasize immediate work placement and limit the clients they assign to training or education.[27]

In addition, other research has established that the com-mon assumption that skills must be learned in school or training programs separate from work is mistaken. That idea reflects middle-class experience, where many people spend years in school or college before they take a regular job. In fact, most workers learn their skills largely at work, not in school or training programs. The best way to elevate one's skills for most people is simply to work steadily in one's current position and move up to more demanding jobs over time. Thus, immediate work attachment need not come at the expense of skills.[28]

The jury is no longer out. Findings from numerous reports unequivocally show better results from the work-first approach as it relates to placement, retention, and wages. Or as Larry Mead put it: "Successful approaches embody the principle that to go to work, one must simply go to work. There is no substitute for taking a job and working out what that requires—on the job. Nothing that a program does can substitute for actual work experience. The program's role, rather, is to get its clients working as quickly as possible and keep them there."[29] Using education and training to upgrade then becomes the next step.

But, in spite of the clear evidence that rapid attachment strategies are most effective, some critics still hold dearly to the mentality that poor people on welfare should not quickly be placed in a job and indeed, even more paternalistically, are not capable of rapid employment. Most notable as of this writing, after 20 years of work-first success in NYC, Mayor de Blasio wants to largely abandon the work-first approach and return to an unsuccessful education and training first approach, along with industry-specific bridge and pathway programs that will likely swell the welfare rolls again and leave people lingering in lengthy preparatory programs that simply delay, but do not truly promote work.

Additionally President Obama announced broad changes in July 2012 that set the stage for a potential retreat on work. He offered states waiver authority to dilute TANF work participation rate requirements in favor of other less enforceable measures—this in spite of the fact that the president had stated on numerous previous occasions that he had no authority under TANF statute to grant such waivers. While increasing state flexibility is always a good idea, this guidance seemed strongly biased toward granting waivers to states who would rely on softer and less clear measures of work rather than those who further emphasized and strengthened the strong work participation rates.[30] Strong opposition in Congress and elsewhere to preserve measurable work requirements in TANF and actual legislative challenges have so far stopped any states from seeking such waivers.

But retreats from strong work requirements such as Mayor de Blasio's new employment plan for New York City and the president's attempt to allow weaker work compliance measures do not bode well for our goal of decreasing poverty in the long run. As Robert Doar, former commissioner of HRA in NYC and now the Morgridge Fellow in Poverty Studies at the American Enterprise Institute, put it in his June 2014 testimony to the House Budget Committee: "Not working is the quickest pathway to poverty in the United States."[31]

And his statement is well substantiated. According to a 2013 US Census Bureau report, in 2012, 60 percent of those in poverty ages eighteen to sixty-four did not work at least one week out of the year. In contrast, the poverty rate for full-time, year-round workers was only 2.9 percent.[32]

There is no reason to delay putting individuals to work by putting them into a training program first—in fact, delaying work can actually cost families money. One crucial benefit of work is it makes families eligible for two significant wage supplements through the federal tax system: the EITC and the child tax credit (CTC). These are in effect negative income taxes, because, to the degree they exceed the amount of taxes owed, they come to the households as a refund check when tax returns are filed. Since most low-income working families owe little or no taxes to begin with, about 87 percent of EITC benefits come in the form of a tax refund. This tax refund amounts to a significant boost to real wages for many low-income families.[33] Both credits are easily accessible by most eligible households because they are redeemed by simply filing out an annual tax return. Additionally, they are only available to working households, garnering strong historical bipartisan support.

In Tax Year 2014, a single parent household raising one child could receive an EITC of up to $3,305. A single parent household raising two children could receive an EITC of up to $5,460. A single parent household raising three or more children could receive an EITC of up to $6,143.[34] Eligible married couples with children receive a somewhat higher EITC, and single or childless couple taxpayers receive a smaller but important wage supplement through the EITC as well. The refundable CTC adds further wage supplementation to households raising children under age seventeen who are claimed as dependents on their tax return.

Russell Sykes, former New York State Deputy Commissioner from 2004 to 2011 and previous Chair of the National Association of State TANF Administrators (NASTA), emphasized a work-first philosophy because "not only was it a good thing for single parent households to escape being on welfare, it also set a positive generational impact for their children. And, once working and receiving the EITC, the CTC, child care subsidies, and other wage supplements, their family income situation was dramatically better." He also noted that New York, one of the twenty-six states with their own EITC, added almost another billion dollars in the aggregate annually to the incomes of low-wage earners, over and above the federal EITC. "Basically, when just looking at the economics, it makes no sense to delay work and become mired in a classroom setting—instead get a job, work hard, take the first step towards a potential career and reap the benefits of all the additional tax supplements that go along with work—upgrading skills and education can still occur after that first step."[35]

So, is there a role for ongoing education and training? Of course, the answer is yes, *but it should come predominantly after a job is secured, not before.* Throughout this book, I've emphasized that "work-first" is our mantra. Bowes and I have fought long and hard to successfully move dependent people into jobs and self-sufficiency. This strategy has worked. Work acculturates, socializes, creates self-esteem, establishes role models for children, and nourishes the soul. And it is equally clear that focusing on raising the level of human capital before work has failed, most often, to pull poor people from dependence to independence. There is no good argument that sitting in a classroom is preferable if a job exists outside.

But, there is a place and a sequence for adding to an individual's skills and education so they might advance up the career ladder, particularly if that first job is not enough to lift the person fully out of poverty. And for those with very limited skills, the best work-first strategies might be either an unpaid work experience placement where the participant works off their TANF grant, usually in a public works program, to acquire the job skills necessary for paid employment or a limited-time subsidized job. Such work experience is defined in a 2008 report by Mathematica Policy Institute as follows: "Unpaid work experience is designed to mirror regular employment in the paid labor market. TANF recipients are assigned to entry-level jobs at government offices, nonprofit agencies, educational institutions, or for-profit businesses, creating an immediate attachment to the labor market. Rather than earning an hourly wage, recipients receive their TANF grant and food stamp benefits in exchange for the hours they work."[36]

In 2014, America Works awarded six fellowships to college graduates interested in adult education. These fellows spent a year working within our company—a phenomenal and successful group. Since bringing these fellows on, the cohort has been expanded with an additional round of nine fellow awards in 2015. In order to accommodate the city's new approach, America Works has gone to its major employers and created curriculum for training before placements. To date, America Works has nine trainings in food safety, OSHA, computer technology, high school equivalency, pre-high school equivalency, customer service, English as a second language, and commercial driving licensing. Finally, with Baruch College's Professor Steve Savas, we designed and run professional development trainings that assist individuals who are excelling on the job learn the skills necessary to rise through the ranks. Both Allied Barton and CVS have helped us put this training in place after seeing the success of our placements in their companies.

All of this training is being researched and evaluated by Swati Desai, former head of research for New York City's Human Resource Administration. Most people have benefited from the classes while they are also performing job search and quite a few are coming into our offices for training after job placement occurs. To date, two thousand one hundred people have participated in the training and people have enjoyed the classes immensely. Employers are impressed with the great industry knowledge graduates demonstrate upon placement.

Beginning in 2014, America Works began a series of contextualized literacy programs. Based upon Desai's research, all programs were designed and directed for our employers. This was premised on the notion that only education programs done in collaboration with employers will ultimately lead to jobs. The results were carefully evaluated. The classes included food handler certificates, customer services, computer skills, commercial drivers license, health care, and security. In addition we offered ESL, high school equivalency, and general education.

The results of the initial classes were significant. In our Brooklyn office there was a 7.3 percent increase in wages. In Queens there was a 13.8 percent increase in employment. Overall, there was a 4.7 percent increase in wages and a 4 percent increase in employment. This was all accomplished within less than a year. As always, regardless of our predilections, we used research to confirm a program's efficacy, in this case a specialized designed education project. This will now be added to the work-first approach of America works.

Subsidized employment or transitional jobs programs subsidize all or part of a wage for a set period of time either directly through the employer or through an intermediary organization, acting on the employer's behalf. When run correctly, this can be a very successful approach and often leads to retention of the client in an unsubsidized job when the subsidy expires. The TANF Emergency Contingency Fund (TECF) stressed subsidized employment as one of three allowable activities for states to receive significant additional dollars under the American Recovery and Reinvestment Act.[37]

In fact, since 2009, thirty-nine states and the District of Columbia have received approval from the HHS–Administration for Children and Families under ARRA to spend $1.3 billion of the TANF Emergency Fund on subsidized employment programs, creating two hundred and sixty thousand jobs in a relatively short period of time. Across the sites, employers reported retaining 37 percent of the subsidized workers after the subsidy period ended.[38] If retention services such as those supplied by America Works' corporate representatives been provided, perhaps that 37 percent would have risen dramatically as it did with us. We saw a well over 55 percent retention since we intervened in what I call the static in the workers' lives—no day care, no housing, an abusive mate at home, and so on.[39] Still, 37 percent is a very respectable rate and clearly demonstrates that these previously unskilled workers received enough on-the-job training to be eligible for full employment.

The failures of job training and education-based programs in the past must not prevent us from considering their place in a strategy to provide jobs instead of dependence. But determining how to structure education, training, and skill development programs, as well as where and by whom they should be provided, requires first answering these fundamental questions: why have they not worked to help people obtain jobs? How can we create training and education that successfully moves people into the jobs that will help them escape poverty? What is the proper role for education and training in a jobs strategy to reduce reliance on government?

First, we must not repeat the mistakes of the past. As we have seen in other parts of this book, poverty programs typically made the error of bypassing and challenging existing institutions, relying instead on poorly run and operated neighborhood organizations. Accountability was sorely lacking. Singularly incompetent teachers and trainers provided little or no serious education. The number of people who have come to America Works having been in multiple training programs beforehand with no job at the end would astound anyone. Yet, the politicians supporting these groups relied on their support in turn at the polls and thus drove funding to them despite negligible results. Any accountability would jeopardize this pas de deux.

The vast amounts of public monies spent did not benefit the clients themselves, but often went solely to the ineffective providers of such services. Yet the ineffective programs continue unaltered and unchallenged.

Second, training has mainly been geared toward jobs that existed at the program's inception but evaporated by program's end, or even worse, for jobs that were never there in the first place. In some ways this mirrors what goes on in public schools in vocational training. For instance, there are file clerk programs and phlebotomist training that lead nowhere for permanent jobs. Outdated equipment used to teach by incompetent teachers for phantom jobs inevitably results in unemployment.

There is a third and vitally important issue. Those in the public sector and the nonprofit world are generally skeptical, disdainful, and suspicious of the private sector. Mostly liberals, they see capitalism as an enemy—as the cause of poverty, not its savior. What would we expect, then, of the programs

they design and run? Just what has happened: a lack of collaboration with employers themselves in the private sector
to design and develop effective programs for the transition
of people into existing jobs.

Now, some of that has changed in America. The failures of
the past have been recognized and in some cases addressed.
Specific job sector-based approaches are finally becoming the
norm, where programs like America Works provide short-
term soft workplace skills coupled with employer partnerships
to directly place clients. Employers themselves, sometimes
in partnership with educational providers and community
colleges, are directly involved in this model by designing ongoing curriculum and teaching more advanced and specific job
skills in the actual or simulated work environment. Instead
of classroom to work where content often has no relationship to existing jobs, this focuses on work-first, and then on
building the skills needed to advance in the workplace and
along a "career pathway."

A recent article in *BusinessWeek* reported that "Employers,
schools, and government agencies are learning to work
together to fill jobs requiring 'middle' skills—more than a
high school diploma but less than a bachelor's degree. The
best community colleges and other training programs are
preparing students for the jobs of today and tomorrow, not
yesterday. They're imparting education when and where students are most likely to absorb it, in keeping with a maxim
of Lou Mobley, who started executive education at IBM:
'Education is effective only at the time of felt need and clear
relevance.'"[40]

The growing trend in workforce development is to have
businesses actually taking the lead in training and skill development, on their own in the workplace or in collaboration
with flexible educational providers such as community
colleges and others. This is an approach that simply makes

far more sense than education and training programs not working with employers and whose approach is divorced from the actual labor market.

Fortunately, many nonprofits have begun to learn from for-profit organizations in the welfare-to-work arena that success ultimately depends on the marketplace and good relationships with employers, as well as respect for and the ability to meet their needs. But change has been slow and progress hard. For a strategy of meaningful education and training to work, nonprofit institutions, for-profit intermediaries, or private companies should be developing new programs. One potential program could employ a marketplace approach in which trainees would have vouchers that they could use to choose the vendor they preferred. These would be available either for basic education and skill training or directed toward upgrading existing skills for increased earnings. Employers would see the added value of allowing and encouraging employees to pursue continued education in addition to work and would be motivated to be involved in actual program and curriculum design.

The object here would be to generate a responsive marketplace that does not require government operation except for the issuing and monitoring of the vouchers. Effective programs would survive and grow while the others would die out, unlike most government-operated programs. The competitive marketplace is more robust in its rewarding success and sun-setting failure.

In thinking about potential programs, we would be wise to listen to Harold Holzer, an American economist, educator, and public policy analyst, who has identified three important factors that combine to help assure successful education and training programs for the disadvantaged: (1) Education and training that gives workers a postsecondary credential; (2) direct ties to employers or industries; and

(3) intervention with workers at the job site to navigate any ongoing issues.

In addition Holzer supports labor market intermediaries (like America Works), who serve to bring together the workers, employers, training providers, and sources of supports needed to make this process work. The use of intermediaries can help with people's on- and offsite issues—the static—that get in the way of success. The intermediaries can also help overcome employer resistance to hiring workers (perhaps owing partly to discrimination) by providing more information on positive worker skills and attributes and by carefully screening the applicants whom they refer to these employers. America Works has staff members called corporate representatives who go to the work site and try to either anticipate problems or deal with existing impediments. Bowes always says that people do not lose their jobs because of what they do not know, but rather because they don't fit in. Helping with life skills and mitigating on and off the job static can often save a willing worker from termination.

The use of the WPA-style subsidized public jobs combined with the upgrading of human capital is just one route to successful independence. Another approach would combine a low paying private-sector job with training or education, ultimately upgrading the worker to a position with wages that no longer require government supplementation. The key here is to link the work to the appropriate schooling. Not doing so has been a major failing of previous efforts.

Such an approach is known as Career Pathways, where short-term sector-based training is provided that allows a combination of work, education, and skill building. New York has operated such a program since 2009. Their request for Career Pathway proposals notes: "programs that combine work, training, and targeted educational activities offer the best employment results for clients transitioning from public assistance to work."[41]

Career Pathways programs have become more prevalent nationwide, but are still underutilized. A recent GAO report encourages broader use of this strategy, as it builds on and adds to successful work-first approaches. Career Pathways programs put welfare recipients to work by working with employers to design short-term education and skill-building curriculum aimed at rapid employment or provide programs that help those leaving welfare for work to acquire additional skills and education on the job site itself. This approach creates a career ladder leading to higher wages over time, either in the original sector or another employment field.[42] An example of this is para-transit. In New York City there are a number of operators of Access-A-ride, providing van transport to the elderly, handicapped, and others, twenty-four hours a day and seven days a week. To become a driver you need to only have a CDL license. In our Bronx office we take anyone with interest and a New York State drivers license and give them a CDL preliminary training program. The company then interviews them and if they pass the interview, they then get qualified with additional training at the employer's site for CDL certification. The first person who went through the program got over fifty hours of work and took home almost $700 on his first week on the job, thanks to an hourly wage of $14.50 for the first forty hours and time and a half after that.

Moreover, research is ongoing into best practices for such programs. A major study of Career Pathways approaches, one of the largest ever undertaken, is currently being funded with both private dollars and grants from the HHS Office of Planning, Research and Evaluation (OPRE). The study, *Innovative Strategies for Increasing Self-Sufficiency*, is a 10-year effort, led by Abt Associates, to evaluate career pathways programs as a strategy for increasing the economic self-sufficiency of low-income individuals and families.[43]

As noted previously, most evaluations of programs to build the elements of education and training for the disadvantaged have shown little or no success. The NEWWS summation of various rigorous studies by Manpower Demonstration Research Corporation (MDRC) and others gives little hope for most such efforts. These studies used the gold standard random assignment approach contrasting a treatment group with a control group. They found starkly that when the treatment group received human capital/education and training programs initially, neither increased employment nor earnings levels occurred above the control group; in fact, little seemed to work.

One of the main failings of employment programs is that little or no heed has been paid to relations with the end hiring companies. Upgrading is conducted in a vacuum divorced from the private sector. No wonder they fail. But in the rare instances where programs act together with private businesses, such as the program run by Cristo Rey, it becomes obvious why the approach being recommended here would likely succeed.

Cristo Rey is a private Catholic school in Harlem that serves high school students from low-income families in urban areas. The program starts in ninth grade, and applicants must be fourteen years old by the beginning of their first year. While enrolled, students are required to work at least five days a month, the proceeds of which go toward their tuition (paying for 70 percent of it). The purpose of the work, as stated on the program Website, is "to fund the majority of his or her education, gain job experience, grow in self-confidence, and realize the relevance of his or her education." The coursework is geared toward college prep, and 100 percent of graduates go on to attend a two- or four-year college. The school also "provides data-driven decision-making to maximize student learning." In the end, these students leave their further education with a leg up for entry into the world of work.

Joe Klein reported in *Time* magazine on a very successful training program for youth on a Navajo reservation in the Southwest. His assessment of the remarkable results was that you must have teachers the trainees like, teach them with vigor, and make the training lead to jobs or recognized certification, often in partnership with businesses. This program taught young people veterinarian skills by doctors. They also taught them the life skills that would get them into advancement to become veterinarians.[44]

Another example, as recounted in Paul Osterman and Beth Shulman's *Good Jobs America* (2011) is Project Quest in San Antonio, TX. It works with employers to identify future job needs and involves the employers in its design and training. It also provides support to the trainees in the form of counseling and some financial aid. When there is a robust coordination between the prospective jobs and the programs, programs that incorporate training and education are successful. This has been shown to work and would be the foundation for building on work-first efforts.

To repeat, my skepticism toward education and training in the past is directed toward ineffective attempts to use it as a first strike in moving dependent people off the dole. I still maintain, based on my fifty years in antipoverty programs, that work-first works best. But here I would temper that statement by acknowledging that, for some, a work-first approach should be combined with ongoing, relevant education and training. This two-pronged approach would help those not yet ready for work become capable of lifting themselves into independence. If vouchers were provided for this, we could assure the quality of the programs over the long run by allowing the marketplace to winnow out the unsuccessful ones.

Further, intermediary organizations, charged with managing the process as well as providing intervention for the static that gets in the way, will assure greater retention in the jobs. Again, as America Works already does, these intermediaries would be paid for performance—placement in well-paying jobs and long-term retention. Private-sector jobs, public-sector jobs—all reinforced by the requisite education and training and then combined with assistance in maintaining the job—would provide a clear path for reduced dependency.

The failures of past education and training programs should not prevent a careful analysis going forward of how these efforts could productively be built into my proposals. There is no need to reject the use of education and training programs altogether if they are designed with an eye toward proper sequencing, the involvement of employers themselves in developing ongoing curriculum and skill training and fully integrated into my call for work and reduced dependency. And if the added education and training helps to lift some further out of poverty, bring it on.

## Notes

1.  Voltaire, *Candide*. Translated by John Butt (New York: Penguin, 1947), 143.
2.  "In 2010, work declined and poverty rose, due to the Great Recession. Yet the combination of relatively high work rates in 2010 (relative to the 1987 to 1993 period) kept poverty lower than during the earlier period." AEU/Brookings Working Group on Poverty and Opportunity, *Opportunity, Responsibility, and Security: A Consensus Plan for Reducing Poverty and Restoring the American Dream* (Washington, DC: American Enterprise Institute and Brookings Institution, 2015), 29.
3.  Gottschalk, Peter, "Can Work Alter Welfare Recipients' Beliefs?," *Journal of Policy Analysis and Management* 24, no. 3 (Summer 2005): 485–98.
4.  Gordon Waddell and A Kim Burton, "Is Work Good for your Health and Well-Being?," https://www.gov.uk/government/

uploads/system/uploads/attachment_data/file/214326/hwwb-is-work-good-for-you.pdf, p. 11.

5.   Ibid., 20.

6.   Lawrence M. Mead, *The New Politics of Poverty: The Nonworking Poor in America* (New York: Basic Books, 1992), chap. 3. Martin Gilens, *Why Americans Hate Welfare: Race, Media, and the Politics of Antipoverty Policy* (Chicago, IL: University of Chicago Press, 1999). Fay Lomax Cook, *Who Should Be Helped? Public Support for Social Services* (Beverly Hills, CA: Sage, 1979).

7.   http://www.latimes.com/science/sciencenow/la-sci-sn-unemployment-depression-risk-20150319-story.html.

8.   The earned income tax credit (EITC) and child tax credit (CTC) are successful federal tax credits for low- and moderate-income working people that encourage work, help offset the cost of raising children, and lift millions of people out of poverty. Chart Book: The Earned Income Tax Credit and Child Tax Credit, Center on Budget and Policy Priorities. http://www.cbpp.org/research/index.cfm?fa=topic&id=27.

9.   Ron Haskins, *Work Over Welfare: The Inside Story of the 1996 Welfare Reform Law* (Washington, DC: Brookings University Press, 2006).

10.  http://aspe.hhs.gov/hsp/newws/5yr-11prog01/index.htm; for the results of the program in Portland, Oregon, see http://www.mdrc.org/sites/default/files/full_391.pdf, p. 28.

11.  Amy Brown, Work First: How to Implement an Employment-Focused Approach to Welfare Reform, MDRC, 1997.

12.  Throughout this chapter, among numerous other sources, points of reference and the evidence of the primacy of "work first" have also been extracted from an unpublished work by Lawrence M. Mead, "America Works: Putting the Poor to Work," 2nd draft (New York: New York University, Department of Politics, October 2012).

13.  Gene Falk, The Temporary Assistance for Needy Families (TANF) Block Grant: A Primer on TANF Financing and Federal Requirements, Congressional Research Service, April 2, 2013; For additional background go to: https://www.fas.org/sgp/crs/misc/RL32748.pdf.

14.  Ron Haskins, *Work Over Welfare: The Inside Story of the 1996 Welfare Reform Law* (Washington, DC: Brookings University Press, 2006).

15.  Lawrence M. Mead, *Beyond Entitlement: The Social obligations of Citizenship* (New York: Free Press, 1986).

16.  See note 156 above.

17.  Irene Lurie, *At the Front Lines of the Welfare System* (New York: The Rockefeller Institute Press, 2006), 130.

18.  Gayle Hamilton and Judith M. Gueron, "The Role of Education and Training in Welfare Reform," Brookings Institution Paper, April 2002.

19.  Gueron and Rolston, *Fighting For Reliable Evidence*; Gayle Hamilton, Stephen Freedman, Lisa Gennetian, Charles Michalopoulos, Johanna Walter, Diana Adams-Ciardullo, Anna Gassman-Pines, Sharon McGroder, Martha Zaslow, Surjeet Ahluwalia, and Jennifer Brooks, with Electra Small and Bryan Ricchetti, *National Evaluation of Welfare-to-Work Strategies: How Effective Are Different Welfare-to-Work Approaches? Five-Year Adult and Child Impacts for Eleven Programs* (New York: Manpower Demonstration Research Corporation, November 2001).

20.  See note 2 above; On the Riverside study: http://www.mdrc.org/sites/default/files/full_96.pdf.

21.  Howard S. Bloom, Carolyn J. Hill, and James A. Riccio, "Linking Program Implementation and Effectiveness: Lessons from a Pooled Sample of Welfare-to-work Experiments," *Journal of Policy Analysis and Management*, 22, no. 4 (Autumn (Fall) 2003): 551–75.

22.  Lawrence M. Mead, "The Primacy of Institutions," *Journal of Policy Analysis and Management* 22, no. 4 (2003): 577–80; Bloom, Hill and Riccio, *Linking Program Implementation and Effects*-2003.

23.  Judith M. Gueron and Howard Rolston, *Fighting For Reliable Evidence* (New York: Russell Sage Foundation, 2013), 351.

24.  http://aspe.hhs.gov/hsp/newws/#TOC.

25.  Hamilton et al., *National Evaluation of Welfare-to-Work Strategies.*

26.  U.S. Department of Health and Human Services Administration for Children and Families Office of the Assistant Secretary for Planning and Evaluation. "The National Evaluation of Welfare-to-Work Strategies: The Experiences of Welfare Recipients Who Find Jobs." By Karin Martinson. December, 2000. P. 10.

27.  The major studies were by the Manpower Demonstration Research Corporation, in New York. In an experimental

evaluation, a sample of individuals from the client population is randomly allocated to either the tested program or a control group. The impact, or effect, of the program is then measured by comparing outcomes for the clients in the experimental program with those for clients in the control group. Because of random assignment, the two groups are highly likely to be equivalent, so that any difference in outcome can be reliably attributed to the program.

28. Robert I. Lerman, "Are Skills the Problem?," in *A Future of Good Jobs? America's Challenge in the Global Economy*, ed. Timothy J. Bartik and Susan N. Houseman (Kalamazoo, MI: Upjohn, 2008), ch. 2.

29. Mead, America Works: Putting the Poor to Work, NYU, 2012, unpublished.

30. http://www.manhattan-institute.org/html/ir_27.htm#. VI7-IWTF_Lc.

31. The War on Poverty at 50: Building on What Works, Reforming What Doesn't, http://budget.house.gov/uploadedfiles/ doar_testimony.pdf.

32. DeNavas-Walt, Carmen; Proctor, Bernadette D.; Smith, Jessica C., "Income, Poverty, and Health Insurance Coverage in the United States: 2012," United States Census Bureau, September 2013, http://www.census.gov/prod/2013pubs/ p60-245.pdf.

33. See: http://www.empirecenter.org/wp-content/uploads/ 2012/04/PB-EITC-041812.pdf. Russell Sykes, Making Work Pay in New York: The Earned Income Tax Credit, Empire Center for New York State Policy, Policy Briefing No. 6, April 2012, Albany, NY.

34. http://eitcoutreach.org/home/tax-credit-information.

35. Discussion with Peter Cove December 2014 and http:// www.empirecenter.org/wp-content/uploads/2012/04/ PB-EITC-041812.pdf.

36. http://www.aspe.hhs.gov/hsp/08/TANFWPR/3/index.shtml.

37. The American Recovery and Reinvestment Act of 2009 created a $5 billion Emergency Contingency Fund for state TANF programs, available in fiscal years 2009 and 2010. Pub.L. No. 111-5, § 2101(a)(1), 123 Stat. 115, 446.

38. Anne Roder and Mark Elliot, Stimulating Opportunity: An Evaluation of ARRA-Funded Subsidized Employment Programs, Economic Mobility Corporation. NY, September 2013, http://economicmobilitycorp.org/uploads/stimulating-opportunity-full-report.pdf:.

39. See Table 1, Introduction of this book.

40. http://www.businessweek.com/articles/2014-11-20/job-training-that-works-where-certificates-replace-degrees#p1.

41. https://otda.ny.gov/contracts/2013/CPII/CPII-RFP.pdf.

42. Temporary Assistance for Needy Families: Action is Needed to Better Promote Employment Focused Approaches, GAO 15-31, November 2014, pages 17–20; http://www.gao.gov/assets/670/667051.pdf.

43. Brendan Kelly and David Fein, *Innovative Strategies for Increasing Self-Sufficiency (ISIS) Project Stakeholder Views from Early Outreach. Rep* (Washington, DC: Office of Planning, Research and Evaluation Administration for Children and Families U.S. Department of Health and Human Services, 2009), Print.

44. http://content.time.com/time/magazine/article/0,9171,2113794-2,00.html.

# 7

# The Road to Work and Reduced Dependency: Real Policy Solutions

*"The only place success comes before work is in the dictionary."*
—Vince Lombardi

All of my experience in fighting poverty tells me that work must replace dependence. We are obliged to create the jobs that will lead people previously dependent on government largesse to self-sufficiency. And so, I am calling for no less than a revolution in fighting poverty—one that can only be accomplished with a seismic shift in the way we now conduct such programs.

My prescriptions are simple, but radical. *No more welfare* except for those who truly cannot work for mental or physical reasons. *No more poverty programs*, which, despite spending over $22 trillion since the mid-1960s, have had no measurable effect on the poverty rates in our country. And then a redeployment of these funds for creating jobs in the private sector and as a last choice, in the public. We will move then from a dependency culture to one of work.

To be clear, government support will come as a supplement to those working or those unable to work. Examples
include day care and health benefits. They will be directed
to individuals and hiring agents—private companies and,
when necessary, public employment. Both Republican and
democratic candidates favor the earned income tax credit
(EITC), as a program that supports the working poor yet
is more than just a handout. What I am proposing, then,
is support for work and if there are some social needs that
must be met, they will be done in the context of a job, not
as a handout for staying at home. Mutual responsibility is
of paramount importance—you work, you will receive the
necessary help to stay in a job.

In the words of President Clinton, welfare as we know it
will end. That means no support for idleness. It does mean
support for those able and willing to enter the workforce. This
will extend the policies of the welfare law of 1996 which made
work a requirement to other government support programs.
One example. That law encourages work requirements for
those on Food Stamps. But it has been weakly enforced and
the Obama administration has discouraged it. Food Stamps
recipients as well as those receiving other government handouts will be required to work.

There are those who will reject this notion, frightened that
eliminating welfare programs without certainty that jobs materialize may end up leaving the vulnerable with no means of support.
I will address this concern further on. For now, I ask the reader
to approach this with an open mind. Yes, it is a paradigm shift,
but one we are morally obligated to consider. I hope you find
the proposals herein worthy of a national dialogue unfettered
by partisan and ideological rhetoric. Once again my mantra is
a simple one: "See not what you know, know what you see."

The plan called for here is suggestive. It is not to be considered a definitive strategy for changing the culture from

dependence to work. Instead, it poses some ways of think-ing about the political necessities required to accomplish this. There may well be disagreements with some of the assumptions in my calculations and challenges to several of my suggested political strategies. This is to be expected. The important thing is that we change the culture of America from one where the government provides the means of dependence to one that focuses on the provision of jobs. And that the withering of the counterproductive and ineffective welfare and poverty programs will finance those jobs. This, more than anything, is a cultural shift in policy. The reader should see this chapter's examples as a beginning in the redirection of funds to help the poor, a sea change in our approach to helping those in need. It is meant to stimulate a rethinking of poverty policy. It is no less than a call to arms for our country's conscience.

That is a debate worth having.

This is what I think of as the "money chapter." It will lay out the assumptions and decisions made to calculate the monetary resources freed by eliminating welfare and pov-erty programs. It will then address how this money will be employed to create jobs. The question is: will there be enough money to create jobs, daycare, and education and training for those previously dependent on the government? The main proposals behind *Work-First* depend entirely on whether this question can be answered in the affirmative. It's necessary to detail the calculations and determine whether there really is enough money to accomplish this.

I propose a different direction for helping many of the poor, a departure from the hodgepodge of income transfer programs to a single guaranteed jobs and income program. It would redirect most of the funding currently going to various transfer benefits and would reinvest those dollars to create millions of new jobs. It would also build upon and expand the EITC and other refundable tax credits to supplement wages, in effect guaranteeing a certain level of income relative to family size. Here is the remarkable transformation if we substituted work for dependence: an impressive 5.65 million jobs could be created at $8.50/hour, predominantly in the private sector along with some transitional jobs in the public sector at a cost of just over $100 billion.[1]

Initial jobs created would go to the 2.35-4.6 million able-bodied nonworking food stamp recipients without dependents,[2] the 900,000 current adult recipients of Temporary Assistance for Needy Families (TANF),[3] and an estimated 25 percent of current SSDI recipients, or 2.2 million individuals, who upon review of their disability diagnosis would be found capable of work[4] after all. These populations would be required to participate in the jobs program. And many more workers would likely emerge from the ranks of the long-term unemployed—those who have given up seeking work, after extended difficulties finding a job. In the end, the goal would be to employ not just aid recipients, but all able-bodied American adults.

The bulk of these jobs would be in the private sector, taking advantage of subsidies to make initial hiring attractive to employer, followed by the negotiated retention that occurs when an employer makes the jobs permanent. This would be a combination of jobs in various sectors such as health, retail, transportation, hospitality, security, and food preparation. Some fractional component would likely also be public works jobs, repairing infrastructure, for instance. But the exact mix of private and public sectors would inevitably be subject to the political temper of the time.

This program would be phased in over the course of five years and provide states with maximum flexibility in the delivery and design of the effort. An evaluation component to be subcontracted through a competitive bid process would be built into the program to provide continuous feedback on success and necessary alterations.

Crucial to this program would be the EITC, which effectively functions as a negative income tax, supplementing real wages in the form of a yearly tax refund. The EITC would be expanded for single and childless couples, and the 2009 changes in the EITC that reduced the marriage penalty and increased the credit for households with three or more children would be made permanent. Combined with the refundable child tax credit, these changes would form the basis of a broader wage supplement program.

A conceptual, varying guaranteed income would be proposed for households of one to five members based on a formula of what a three-person household currently receives from a combination of $8.50 hourly wages, food stamp benefits, and the federal EITC, which equates to $29,272 annually (see Figure 7.1).

Many states already have state EITCs, which further expand total income for a household with a wage earner at $8.50/hour, and others could similarly implement a state EITC or other wage supplements.

**Figure 7.1.** Proposed guaranteed income based on household size.

| Supplemental income thresholds—revised 12/11/14 | | | | |
| --- | --- | --- | --- | --- |
| Persons per family | 1 person | 2 person | 3 person | 4 person |
| Family size adjustment (percent of base) | 58.8% | 79.4% | Base | 120.6% |
| Income threshold | $ 17,261.00 | $ 23,267.00 | $ 29,272.00 | $ 35,277.00 |

Note: Created by America Works of New York, Inc. Reprinted with permission.

Managing a program that sets a goal of creating and funding 5.65 million jobs over its first five years will be a substantial undertaking to say the least. Governance of this jobs program would be under the guidance of a new public–private partnership oversight authority similar to how such arrangements currently function in regard to infrastructure projects. For adult workers with children, additional subsidized child care slots would be added and additional training provided for informal and/or relative care providers.[5]

The vast array of current education and training programs include forty-seven programs spread across nine separate agencies (HHS, DOE, DOL, and elsewhere) at an annual cost of $18 billion.[6] Under this plan these programs would be consolidated under the auspices of a new Cabinet agency that would work closely with the business community to define training modules for soft skills, middle skills, and ongoing on-the-job-training career advancement skills that directly relate to available jobs. I estimate that new efficiencies from central administration and elimination of duplicate programs could save $5 billion. At the present, this is an educated guess. The amounts could rise or be somewhat less.

Financing for the new program could come from multiple sources, including redirecting some funds from the Supplemental Nutrition Assistance Program (Food Stamps), the Women, Infants, and Children program, a 25 percent reduction in SSDI funding, limiting the maximum duration of annual unemployment insurance benefits to thirteen weeks, reduced funding of the federal TANF block grant and state maintenance-of-effort (MOE) funds for non-child-only cases, savings from the Low Income Home Energy Assistance Program, and combining the dollars from the EITC and other tax credits to fund a unified more extensive refundable tax credit/wage supplementation program.

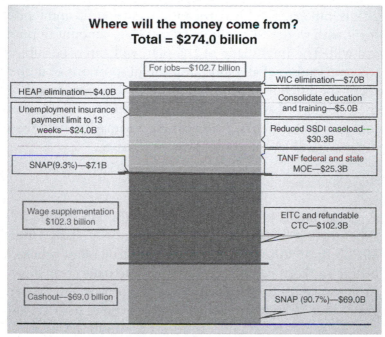

**Figure 7.2.** Where will the money come from?
Note: Created by Bob Scardamalia. Reprinted with permission.

## Work Programs to Be Established

The funds are there, as Figure 7.2 demonstrates: $102.7 billion can be set aside for wage supplementation, if you account for the existing EITC and refundable child tax credit. Another $102.7 billion emerges from the elimination of WIC, HEAP, TANF, just shy of 10 percent of SNAP, and savings from reductions in education and training, unemployment insurance, and a reduced SSDI caseload—this can go directly toward jobs, both public–private and purely public. The remaining 90 percent of SNAP can be cut to produce an extra $69 billion, to be allocated as the political situation dictates.

It is important to stress: the task of cutting aid and replacing it with work will require a tremendous amount of political will. The final shape of the plan will surely be subject to compromises of all kinds, and the proportions of money spent on different programs will inevitably shift, based on the coalitions that will need to be forged to pass this plan into law. Nevertheless, it is possible to imagine how these programs will look and function, in practice.

*Wage Supplementation*

A crucial model for this plan is an existing $14 million subsidy program funded with federal stimulus dollars. Under ARRA, from 2009 to 2012, wage supplementation helped businesses keep people employed and actually created jobs in the wake of the financial crisis. Unfortunately, the program can't be built upon—these funds expired in 2012, and though some states and localities have used TANF block grant funds on modest wage subsidies, most such programs are scattered and highly underfunded. Allocating $102.7 billion, following the template of this model, would have an enormous effect on tackling our seemingly intractable unemployment problem.

Here's how it works: a staffing company places job seekers in temporary positions and subsidizes their wage. These subsidies vary as to the percentage and are usually negotiated with each employer. They can be 100 percent for some period and decline to a lower level or they can start at a lower level usually anywhere from 80 percent down to 50 percent. They also vary in duration, usually no less than ninety days to six months and no more than one year. The durations are to mitigate against employers using subsidy funds to avoid unsubsidized hires. Negotiations on subsidies with employers in most instances include an agreement to hire the person on a permanent basis after some agreed-upon period and depending on satisfactory performance during the subsidy period. This effectively provides an employer with a trial employment period prior to providing permanent employment. The employer runs little or no risk during the period of subsidized employment because the staffing company is the employer of record. The staffing company completes all paperwork involved in the program. The employer may terminate the arrangement at any time.

This means that the employer sees applicant from the staffing company as no different from an outside applicant, except that the net wage cost is lowered by the amount of the subsidy during the trial period. Companies have flocked to the program because of the streamlined process and because they do not have to wait for payment.

Only if the worker stays for ninety days in the job can the staffing company receive the full reimbursement for its services from the state. This assures a high retention rate. Those familiar with the private sector understand that a worker that has been at a company for four to six months, and is producing adequately, is a valuable employee and will be retained. By subsidizing wages in a user-friendly program, companies can stave off layoffs and even pay more than the minimum wage. As well, jobs have been created by companies now able to bring on new employees because costs have been dramatically reduced. Considering the scale of $102.7 billion per year in funding, the implications for job retention and creation in the private sector are eye-popping.

*Infrastructure Creation through Public–Private Partnerships*

Virtually no one would argue with the assertion that our country has neglected to keep our infrastructure up to date. Bridges collapse, roads go unrepaired, mass transit lags perilously behind that of so many other countries, and many of our airports need considerable upgrading. The list is long, but these critical repairs remain low on the list of public expenditures. I propose a massive public works initiative to both address our infrastructure needs and help create jobs. Congress and the states would allocate funds for the projects, which would be administered through public–private partnerships. (The exact nature of this allocation would be subject to the political exigencies of the congress passing this idea into law—though the best and likeliest outcome would surely feature the vast majority of the $102.7 billion funding public–private partnerships that would create jobs that, with EITC expansion, would hit the guaranteed income targets.) The companies responsible for the delivery would be required to hire at least 25 percent of their workforce from those previously receiving government aid.

A successful public–private partnership must have several elements. It must have equitable risk allocation between the parties involved in the partnership. The government must oversee the project in a just and fair way, ensuring the contract and designing and directing the project to meet constituent needs. Additionally, the process must be transparent and fair, and those selected for the partnership must all be evaluated on the same basis. The project also has to be economically viable to attract private-sector investors, and finally, the financial market must be there to invest in the project. If a public–private partnership is missing any of these key elements, it is doomed for trouble.

Public–private partnerships occur in two basic formats. The two formats are build–operate–transfer (BOT) and build–own–operate (BOO). The BOT format occurs when the public sector gives land or existing infrastructure to private interests to carry out a task desired by the public sector. The private entities then build the desired product and operate it for a given period, during which they hope to make a profit, after which they return the property to the public sector to continue operation. An example would be the construction of a bridge by a private company who would then operate it, netting all profits from the tolls for a set period before returning the property to the local government. The BOO model is similar to the BOT model, but the private entities retain control over the project indefinitely. An example would be the construction of a sewer system that the private entity owns and operates in perpetuity.

Public–private partnerships can take almost any form. In Mumbai, India, a partnership was created to build a workforce to help reduce waste by picking recyclables out of the trash. In Bangladesh, a partnership was created to help pay for girls to attend school who would have been otherwise unable to do so. Mexico City partnered to expand their mass transit system, more than tripling the size and capacity of the current system. In Nairobi, Kenya, a partnership was created to provide lighting in slum areas with the purpose of creating a safer environment, which also created advertising space for private companies. In short, public–private partnerships can be utilized to fill any societal need.[7]

Public–private ventures do come with risks. First, can the project be completed to the correct specifications, on time, and on budget? Second, will the product be used and operated in a fashion that meets the original agreement? And finally, will the product create the projected revenue?

Public–private partnerships actually tend to perform better than the usual publicly funded projects. According to separate studies completed in the United States, the United Kingdom, Australia, and Canada, public–private ventures not only were completed on time more often, but were under budget more often as well.[8] A public–private partnership was even able to reduce the current cost of tuberculosis tests by 40 percent.[9]

Public–private partnerships have one further advantage. They tend to gain bipartisan support and allow both nonprofits and private businesses alike to work toward the goals set by the government. This distinguishes them from public jobs, which inevitably carry a whiff of "big government," making them decidedly unpalatable to fiscal conservatives. Nevertheless, some component of this plan will inevitably have to include purely public jobs.

*Public Jobs*

As a last resort, if a person cannot be absorbed by companies through basic demand, wage supplementation or in jobs for infrastructure creation, a modest public jobs alternative would be created. I know many on the right will blanch at this proposal. When I mentioned the whole plan I had to Congressman Paul Ryan he said, "Don't talk to conservatives about public work programs." I would answer this with the following question, "Would we rather have people working, not jobless and on dependency payments than in some publicly created jobs? And further, as conservatives, would they not like the reduction in public expenditures to bring this about. Sure, many work programs have been badly run. But as I have suggested, there are ways to avoid this."

There are examples, such as the WPA or jobs created by the federal highway projects, which prove that public jobs can be effectively created. Unlike the WPA, the creation of these jobs would be contracted to private companies to assure success. The creation of these jobs could be at nonprofits or in public agencies. They would be temporary and linked to job-seeking agencies.

## How to Achieve the Change

The coin of the realm in politics used to be patronage—jobs for the faithful. To a minor extent it still is, but the good government advocates traded much of that for civil service, which began on a federal level in the late nineteenth century. This resulted in the offer of jobs being replaced by entitlements, cash, and favors that were promised for loyal support toward election. As patronage waned and machine politics withered, more and more financial aid and government services became the capital doled out for votes rather than employment.

The political strategy to accomplish the transformation from dependency to work will be based on making the offering of jobs more attractive to politicians than allocating more money to keep people dependent. A new form of patronage will be created to secure politicians' support for reduced welfare and poverty programs.

The model used by America Works has already worked wonders with affecting welfare policy. With welfare, first we ran programs and did research that proved that work-first—not education and training—was the best first strike in moving people off dependency and into employment. We then approached a like-minded think tank, in this case the Progressive Policy Institute, which was an arm of the Democratic Leadership Council. The DLC's first president was Bill Clinton, at the time still governor of Arkansas. The DLC publicized the model we were promoting through writings and conferences. When their executive director, Bruce Reed, became President Clinton's domestic policy adviser we were given direct access to the policy-making at the White House around welfare reform.

We had also begun to brief Newt Gingrich, who was negotiating a welfare bill as House Speaker with Clinton. Gingrich loved the private-sector approach and the work-first model. With both sides in favor of what we believed the best route to reduce dependency, it found its way into the final landmark welfare legislation known as the Personal Welfare and Work Opportunity Act of 1996. The provision for work-first, education and training after, had as much as anything else to cause an over 50 percent reduction in the welfare rolls over a decade.

The first step will be a campaign to heighten public awareness about the issue, using think tanks and the media to make an urgent call for these proposals. Forums and presentations will be in order for getting the message out to policy-makers. Briefings of politicians on key committees would take place. The goal will be to get the issue into the public discourse and to increase the awareness that work is preferable to dependence. The fundamental question asked will be, wouldn't we rather see existing resources support work rather than idleness and dependence? It will be important to frame this issue as neither mean nor punitive. Some opponents will inevitably attempt to position it that way. As Arthur Brooks has warned, the right tends to lose in such sensitive debates since it presents rational arguments and facts while the left appeals to emotion, which wins the day. The public campaign, then, must emphasize that the trade-off is for work and the tenets our country was founded on, in lieu of the degrading condition of dependence. What is being taken away is debilitating and what is being offered is a path to independence—something to which we all aspire.

The key to the success of the plan will be a slow rollout targeting specific welfare programs for elimination or reduction. The disability systems seem ripe as a first attempt to bring about the systemic change I am suggesting.

It will be hugely important that this process of dismantling welfare and poverty programs not simply become a bait and switch. There might be some who see this as a way to reduce state and federal budgets by ending direct assistance to people, but then not replace welfare with jobs. The first safeguard is to include the elimination of welfare and the new jobs program together in the same bill, and to extend it for as many years as possible. This is what happened in the Wisconsin program W-2 in its enactment in 1997. It achieved for one state-level program (AFDC) exactly what we would be looking for on a national level. It retained the welfare allotment received from the feds and required that it all be earned in actual employment or work experience programs akin to WPA. In this way the money could not be redirected to something else.

State or federal constitutional guarantees also must be satisfied. The New York State constitution, for example, is periodically cited as a deterrent under its clause that "the aid, care and support of the needy are public concerns and shall be provided by the state" to declare that housing is a right. So a second safeguard, state by state, would be to incorporate a constitutional restructuring. Given the sweep and magnitude of my proposition, it is not inconceivable that states would find it acceptable to substitute a work program guaranteed by their own constitution.

Equally important, the redirected funds must be placed into a federal trust fund that cannot be used for other purposes. The feds do this already for state funds they collect under the law to pay unemployment claims. These earmarked funds cannot be redirected elsewhere.

The work program itself would be structured as a federal entitlement program like Social Security rather than a discretionary program like the Workforce Investment Act. The entitlement would rely upon a formula that combines wages at $8.50 per hour through what would initially be a subsidized job, in most instances converting into a permanent job, further supplemented by an enhanced EITC. The virtue of creating such programs as an entitlement is that they tend to run forever: they are hard to get rid of and they do not have to be reauthorized by Congress each year. What this accomplishes is to prevent a bait and switch—something the left would fear. If we are going to take away welfare and poverty programs, then we need to protect the alternative I propose. This is one way to guarantee that.

A final way is to turn the funds into a contractual arrangement with the citizens, enforced by the courts. Currently the bloated public pension system cannot easily be trimmed for workers for whom the contract was made, for example, as with teacher union-negotiated defined-benefit plans. The courts have upheld these. There are some cases where cutbacks in pensions have occurred, but they are small.

## Why Work-First Will Work

Just over $100 billion can go a long way. It can subsidize the hiring of workers in hospitals, cashiers in retail, drivers, janitors, security officers, waiters, and line cooks. Once these new workers have the chance to prove themselves on the job, adding enough value to more than make up for the initial subsidy, odds are they will become accepted as permanent, unsubsidized workers. Meanwhile, a small fraction of that $100 billion will be applied directly to public jobs, employing the construction workers, planners, and laborers needed to revitalize our country's aging infrastructure. In this way $100 billion can create 5.65 million jobs, revolutionizing our national approach to poverty. These add up on paper, but I've also consulted with real-world experts who confirm that the model will work as intended. One of these is Jason Turner, former Commissioner of Welfare under Mayor Giuliani.

When I asked Turner to review my proposal, he was categorical in his support—he believed that economically, budgetarily, morally, and socially, it would be a home run. He observed that the prospect of jobs for all guarantees an increase in the gross national product, an increase in wealth for all Americans, not just those who live off of transfers from the government. Likewise, it reduces the net tax burden on working Americans. It can provide for significant improvements in urban communities by creating jobs where there are currently few to be had. Finally, it promotes self-reliance—something our society could use a lot more of. Turner confirmed that the plan is the *only* plan that can be counted on to actually change the personal and financial circumstances of those in need.[10]

Since the War on Poverty began, there has been a mountain of research over the decades on the subject of how best to increase employment and reduce poverty among the welfare population. Soon after the War on Poverty was up and running, Health and Human Services sponsored a large-scale experiment to test the idea as to whether income transfers in which some families received fairly generous unrestricted cash benefits (via a negative income tax) and a control group that did not, to see what the positive or negative effects would be. This experiment showed that those receiving the unrestricted welfare benefits worked significantly fewer hours and experienced higher levels of family dissolution than those in the control group.[11] In other words, free money without obligations resulted in bad social consequences.

Unquestionably, the American work ethic is built into our cultural DNA. Work, not dependency, is the choice most would make. The solution is less complex than the funding and administration of the hundreds of existing welfare and poverty programs we have now. From my discussions with those on both the left and the right, there is a consensus that, if executed with skill, this will solve the problem of poverty and return our citizens to work. This alone should garner the allies necessary to bring about this radical proposal.

Work has always been the best path out of poverty and to a better, more independent life. Belief in the social and economic value of work used to be a shared political philosophy on both sides of the aisle. But now, with the advent of a pervasive dependency culture, too many able-bodied individuals who could be working find themselves instead on

TANF, SNAP, SSDI, HEAP, Unemployment Insurance, and other transfer programs. These transfer benefits, particularly SNAP and HEAP, are often earmarked solely for specific purchases, which is paternalistic and does not allow for households to make normal budgeting decisions, as we all must, if other needs are paramount at the time.

Too many people with manageable disabilities, including depression and back pain, have succumbed to viewing Social Security Disability Insurance as a long-term unemployment program. Many whose welfare has run out have moved onto the disability rolls. With the help of a growing legal industry that excels in maximizing disability claims, and administrative law judges who are in many cases compelled by the federal government to be extraordinarily lenient, far too many individuals have left the workforce at significant taxpayer cost and to their own long-term economic detriment. The number of former workers now participating in the Social Security Disability Insurance has grown from 5.04 million in 2000 to 8.94 million in 2013, a growth rate of 77.5 percent.[12] It is reasonable to assume that through a rigorous case re-review process as many as 25 percent of these individuals could return to work.

And yet in spite of the proliferation of these programs, poverty rates remain high. Without the wages of able-bodied adults in poor households, all of these programs remain insufficient. The percent of people in poverty stands at 14.5 percent in 2013, only slightly lower than the 15.2 percent rate thirty years ago in 1983. During that thirty-year period the percentage has ranged between a low of 11.3 percent in 2000 to a high of 15.2 percent in 1983, but has steadily increased or remained stagnant since 2000.[13] However, when wages, even at slightly above the current minimum wage, are part of the equation, the situation changes. Other supports such as the EITC kick in and there is more progress against poverty.[14] Work, not welfare, is what gets people out of poverty.

In fact, President Franklin D. Roosevelt, architect of the New Deal, stated: "The lessons of history. . . . show conclusively that continued dependence upon relief induces a spiritual and moral disintegration fundamentally destructive to the national fiber. To dole out relief in this way is to administer a narcotic, a subtle destroyer of the human spirit."

This is the essence of the work-first plan: by cutting $270 billion in welfare, aid, SSDI, and dependency of varying types and programs, we can create just over $100 billion for jobs, both public–private and purely public, an additional $100 billion to supplement EITC, improving the real take-home pay of these new workers, and bringing 5.65 million able-bodied adults back into the workplace, out of welfare and dependency.

Partly as a result of this large-scale experiment, along with general public dissatisfaction with welfare, the Congress passed the Family Support Act in 1988, an education and training program intended to move recipients to work, and based on the premise that welfare adults would qualify for jobs and accept them if they were provided additional education and training to improve their skill levels. However, experience showed that the new provision of education and training did not have this effect. In fact the opposite occurred from what had hoped—in the first five years after the program was activated in 1989, rather than declining, the caseload *increased by one-third* to its highest level ever.[15]

Faced with these disappointing results, HHS conducted a multistate, multiyear comparison of the effectiveness of the education and training model embedded in its existing Family Support Act against a work-first intervention, otherwise known as a Labor Attachment model. Under the work-first approach, welfare recipients are encouraged to get into the labor force as soon as they can find a job and improve their employment and wage circumstances from there—as opposed to the skills model where they remain out of the labor force while undergoing remedial education and training.

As we've already seen, the results unequivocally favored the work-first model. The multiyear extensive independent research experiment concluded:

> [Employment-focused] programs generally had larger effects on employment, earnings and welfare receipt than [education-focused] programs. Given the large number of programs examined and their variety of served populations, implementation features, and labor markets, these results provide more support for the advantages of employment-focused programs than for education-focused ones.[16]

In the resulting enacted TANF program, the Congress allocated funds to states with substantial operational flexibility but with the understanding that states must place an increasing number of adult recipients into employment or work-related activities.

Those like Jason Turner who have worked in public policy have seen first-hand that a full-employment universal work activation model such as I propose in this book is operationally feasible. It builds upon the successful TANF approach to work activation as a condition of benefits. While my approach differs from TANF in that it goes much further—after all, it is a *universal* full-employment model—it uses the same work-first orientation which has proven effective as TANF, but on a much larger scale.

Why has required participation in work activity as a condition of benefits proven effective? Part of the reason is that many long-term welfare recipients have accommodated their lives to low levels of income available from the social welfare system, and they do not respond immediately to available higher income levels through work. Many or most of the inactive recipients will benefit by rules and obligations which engage them in work activation, where they *learn how to work by doing work*. The resulting necessary work habits, such as reliability, getting along with co-workers, accepting direction from supervisors, and returning to work day after day, can only be learned by practicing them. My universal work plan is the best option for large-scale adoption of the work habits and skills necessary for success in the private workplace. And we have seen from the success of the less extensive TANF program that such work activation, in practice, leads to sizeable increases in employment and earned income.

Much has been written about the culture of poverty, but it resides not where you might think or where researchers and commentators have looked. Most discussions of this focus on the people mired in material misery and helplessness. Intelligence and moral lassitude head a list of reasons people remain stuck in their world of want. From my almost fifty years working in poverty programs, though, I suggest this is looking from the wrong end of the telescope.

Rather than dissecting the demand side, I suggest the supply side—government and its programs to alleviate poverty—may well be the more likely perpetuator of continuing and increased dependency and want. If you look at the culture of poverty as a result of the unintended consequences of public policy, as I have argued above, then the blame falls less on the victims but on intrusive and destructive government programs.

Let's visit the market of supply by the government. These arrive in the marketplace for the poor in two forms. First, in the provision of goods and services to those who cannot fend for themselves. Second, in the disincentives that make work a poor choice for the poor.

Starting with Roosevelt's New Deal but moved to warp speed by Lyndon Johnson and the War on Poverty, the government goodies lavished on our society have become enormous and ever so insidious in their effect of encouraging dependency. As we have seen in other chapters, in many cases the rational choice is to remain on the myriad subsidies rather than go to work. Why would someone take a job when he could be supported with Food Stamps, housing allowances, Medicaid, welfare, and so many of the other safety net programs available for those not working.

Recently, the Secretary for Work and Pensions for the Cameron government in the United Kingdom visited us. He made an interesting observation. People, he said, say that America has done welfare reform. He demurred. Not so. "Most of the U.S.'s welfare programs have no work requirement, unlike what we are moving to in England." This is so true. As mentioned in this book, the Obama administration came to New York City and told officials they could not require food stamp recipients to work. Official after official talking to welfare recipients at classes we have run have been told that their case workers advised them to go home, have more babies, and collect more money. Again, if only they were aware, the public would be revolted by this.

It is the culture of the government's approach to poverty that is the real culprit. When we scrutinize the growth of dependence in the country, the immediate response is to shine the light on those who benefit from this. But a more rational one would be to ask what is the government doing to propel and perpetuate this growth? This is a chicken and egg situation in which the government is in control of the largesse and the takers are willing stooges.

Charles Krauthammer, a Pulitzer Prize-winning syndicated columnist, political commentator, and physician, warns of the breakdown of mediating institutions between the citizen and government. In his *Washington Post* opinion column, Krauthammer suggests that:

> [ . . . ] to say that all individuals are embedded in and the product of society is banal . . . equating society with government, the collectivity with the state. Of course we are shaped by our milieu. But the most formative, most important influence on the individual is not government. It is civil society, those elements of the collectivity that lie outside government: family, neighborhood, church, Rotary club, PTA, the voluntary associations that Tocqueville understood to be the genius of America and source of its energy and freedom.
>
> Moreover, the greatest threat to a robust, autonomous civil society is the ever-growing Leviathan state.[17]

Recently I heard Krauthammer speak and I believe these were his sentiments. As the state adopts more and more of the responsibility to provide the goods and services previously offered by civil society, it has placed the individual naked before the government. With no intermediary institutions to provide and protect, tyranny is not far behind.

We have become a nation of takers aided and abetted by government. Once honored, work has become an endangered species replaced by government largesse. In this day and age the state can no longer serve as the provider of first resort. It must allow for the means for independence, and that is jobs. And those jobs will allow for people to make their own choices and gain the sense of self-fulfillment, self-reliance, and spiritual attainment that work provides. We owe our citizens no less than that. Now is the time to reverse the perverse trends I have outlined. It is time to end poverty. It is time for us to work at work. It is time to be poor no more.

## Notes

1.   Calculation based on $8.50 × 40 hours × 52 weeks = $17,680; $17,680 × 5.65 million jobs = $100 billion.

2.   Able-bodied Adults Without Dependents, http://www.fns.usda. gov/snap/able-bodied-adults-without-dependents-abawds

3.   U.S. Department of Health and Human Services Office of Children and Families, Caseload Data 2013, May 2014; http:// www.acf.hhs.gov/programs/ofa/resource/caseload-data-2013

4.   Annual Statistical Report on the Social Security Disability Insurance Program, 2012. Rep. no. 13-11826. Washington, DC: Social Security Administration, 2012. Print. Calculated from the Social Security Administration's 2012 Annual Statistical Report on the Social Security Disability Insurance Program (SSDI) at 25 percent of $142.8 billion in annual SSDI benefit outlays FY 2013. Social Security Administration: Budget Issues, Congressional Research Service, March 2013.

5.   Karen Lynch, *The Child Care and Development Block Grant: Background and Funding*, Congressional Research Service, September 27, 2012. Current federal and state child-care funding stems from the Child Care and Development Block Grant and the mandatory funding to states often referred to as the Child Care Entitlement to States. Together these two streams comprise what is known as the Child Care Development Fund (CCDF). Funding from the CCDBG is approximately $2.3–$2.4 billion annually and the Entitlement Funding to States is just over $2.9 billion, for a total of $5.2–$5.3 billion. Adding an additional $1 billion in subsidy funding to states would increase the availability of both center based and informal/formal family day care.

6.   Employment and Training Programs: Opportunities Exist for Improving Efficiency, Testimony of Andrew Sherril, Director of Education, Workforce and Income Security, US Government Accountability Office, Before the House Subcommittee on Labor, Health, Human Services, Education and Related Agencies, April 7, 2011, http://www.gao.gov/new.items/d11506t.pdf.

7.   Josephine D'Allant, "Public-Private Partnerships for Shared Prosperity: It's Working!," *The Huffington Post*, TheHuffingtonPost. com, November 11, 2013. Web. January 19, 2015.

8.  Charles Lammam and Hugh MacIntyre, "A Route to Better Roads: The Case for Public-Private Partnerships – AEI," AEI. American Enterprise Institute, June 11, 2013. Web. January 19, 2015.

9.  "Public-Private Partnership Announces Immediate 40 Percent Cost Reduction for Rabid TB Test." UnitAid.eu. UnitAid, August 6, 2012. Web. January 19, 2015.

10. Personal correspondence with Jason Turner, July 20, 2014.

11. Overview of the Final Report of the Seattle-Denver Income Maintenance Experiment; HHS, 1983.

12. Annual Statistical Report on the Social Security Disability Insurance Program, 2013, Social Security Administration, SSA Publication No. 13-11826, December 2014, Table 1, http://www.ssa.gov/policy/docs/statcomps/di_asr/2012/di_asr12.pdf.

13. U.S. Bureau of the Census Historical Poverty Data – People, Table 2, http://www.census.gov/hhes/www/poverty/data/historical/people.html.

14. Thomas Gabe, *Welfare, Work, and Poverty Status of Female-Headed Families with Children: 1987–2009* (Washington, DC: Congressional Research Service, July 15, 2011).

15. Gene Faulk, *Temporary Assistance for Needy Families (TANF): Size and Characteristics of the Cash Assistance Caseload. Rep. no. 7-5700* (Washington, DC: Congressional Research Service, 2016), Print.

16. Gayle Hamilton, Stephen Freedman, Lisa Gennetian, Charles Michalopoulos, Johanna Walter, Diana Adams-Ciardullo, and Anna Gassman-Pines. National Evaluation of Welfare-to-Work Strategies. MDRC: Building Knowledge to Improve Social Policy. Manpower Demonstration Research Corporation, Dec. 2001. Web. 9 Aug. 2016.

17. Charles Krauthammer, "Charles Krauthammer: Did the State Make You Great?" *Washington Post*, 19 Jan. 2012. Web. 09 Aug. 2016.

# Afterword: 250 Broadway, New York City, Summer 2009

Forty-four years had passed since I last found myself at 250 Broadway. This time, I had been invited to testify in front of the New York City Council. The subject was welfare policy, and many on the council were determined to repeat the mistakes of the past by forcing the city to adopt education and training as a first strike in welfare reduction. We had seen that fail over and over. Yet my colleagues continued to try the same programs.

So here I was at a hearing on welfare policy and listening to testimony supporting the failed policies of the past. The chair of the committee was our now New York City Mayor Bill de Blasio. When I finished my somewhat impassioned opposing testimony he turned to me and said, "That was really good, Peter. But I totally disagree with you." He was supremely gracious, but I knew he was wrong.

America Works had had significant impact on the Clinton White House, Speaker Newt Gingrich, and Congress in convincing them to adopt work-first as the strategy of choice in the 1996 welfare bill. By the time of my testimony, over 60 percent of the welfare rolls had been cut nationwide using work-first. Yet here were the council members arguing with me that education and training were what was now needed. I wondered, had the almost forty-five years since I first visited 250 Broadway taught us nothing? Why the stonewall of resistance to contrary evidence?

Politics often trumps the good. And, as written by William Rathbone Greg in his *Enigmas of Life* (1874): "in this world, a large part of the business of the wise is to counteract the efforts of the good." The potent mixture of politicians trying to do good, responding to constituents also trying to do good, quite often results in the bad. Yet one would ask, why would good people, elected and trying to do right, more often do wrong? It is mystifying to me that there is a growing mantra for Progressives that welfare reform has failed. Despite the evidence, the liberal canard that it has is growing. Have we learned nothing?

Nathan Glazer has written in his *The Limits of Social Policy* (1988) that the liberal answer to every problem is a new program to solve it. And as we have seen, in our attempts to do good, to be benevolent, we have more often than not prescribed panaceas that have had the opposite of the intended effect. Writer and philosopher David Stove has suggested that "the great majority of things are worse done by the intervention of government, than the individuals most interested in the matter would do them, or cause them to be done, if left to themselves." As Andrew Irvine writes in his introduction to Stove's book *What's Wrong with Benevolence* (2011): "In short, Stove's law of unforeseen consequences and Mill's law of individual responsibility together help form something of a bridge between traditional conservatism and traditional liberalism. By minimizing the role of government we maximize our protection against individual calamity. By maximizing individual responsibility we minimize the effect of unforeseen harmful consequences." The difference between Stove's benevolence and our present-day liberal posture should be pointed out. Fred Siegel has pointed out to me that Stove saw benevolence as paternalistic. Present-day benevolence sees the poor as one with those offering help. Just as Sviridoff approached poor people as the victims of oppression the remedies reflected this view of benevolence. The rise of a victim society with its attendant law suits confirms this.

One wonders if those who have faced the social pathologies of a progressively worsening welfare state would have been better served by benign neglect from the start.

My journey from the world of promise and potential to the limits of social policy and its unintended consequences has been sobering. One turns from the shattering of a dream of what could be. I hope that this does not mean the end of our attempts to make a better world for the less fortunate. Surely, getting welfare recipients jobs is not a bad thing.

But the Chair of the City Council I testified before was to become the current mayor in New York. And he has begun to implement some of the Council Committee's proposals. No more hamburger flippers. A high paid job for all through classroom training. This new roll of the dice will be fascinating to watch as we compare its results to the past efforts. Perhaps some of these new policies will help. It may well be that a "kinder, gentler" welfare employment policy will be effective and people will go on to better jobs. But all the evidence says otherwise. Back-pedaling into a modern-day benevolence is repeating a failed approach. Education and training should be add-ons to work as avenues to career advancement not substitutes for work. Otherwise it is a faith-based approach that may well hurt those who are poor.

Then again, the mood of the public, and of those elected to represent them, is always changing. Though it may have swung in favor of our current president and mayor, I have hope that it will continue to turn in favor of those who will use their power to change the way that we fight poverty for the better. I can only think back to something my mentor George Bennett used to say. Whenever we would find ourselves in a dodgy situation, he would tell me to "keep playing the piano." What did he mean by this? Remember the old western movies and a fight would break out in the bar? As everyone was whopping on each other, the piano player would just keep playing and playing, until things calmed down. Well, that sums up my approach to the profession I've plied—through changing times I've just kept playing the piano. Enemies and competitors have mostly disappeared while we have continued to show up every day and tinkled the ivories. Given enough time, the tune will change, and this country might just be ready to be poor no more.

Finally, an old friend once said "If Peter Cove's house were burning down, he would be thankful for the warmth." My glass half full, I believe my proposals will fall on receptive ears and ultimately their prescriptions will be followed.

# Index

CPSIA information can be obtained
at www.ICGtesting.com
Printed in the USA
LVOW13s2320020317
526015LV00031B/703/P